THE OVERLAND LIMITED

SAN DIEGO Howell-North Books CALIFORNIA

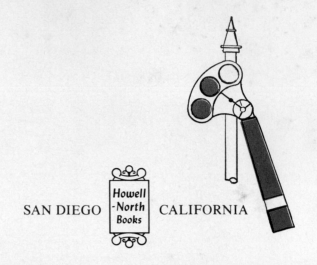

The Overland Limited

BY LUCIUS BEEBE

Acknowledgments

The pictorial and factual material required for the assembling of this monograph derived from a wide variety of sources, some of them amateur collectors and experts in the field of railroad transport of great generosity, others state and official repositories of such matters and the carriers whose fortunes were bound up with those of *The Overland Limited* and still others commercial dealers in stock photographs and the iconographic record of the American past. They include Arthur D. Dubin, Alfred W. Johnson, Fred Jukes, Howard Fogg, Stan Repp, Richard Kindig, Richard Steinheimer, Dr. Philip Hastings, William Kratville, Everett De Golyer, Douglas C. Wornom, Jim Ady, D. L. Joslyn, L. Jackson Welsh, Grahame Hardy, Mrs. Victor Maxwell, The American Geographical Society, The Colorado College Library, Maynard Parker, *The Monterey Herald*, S. S. Pierce & Co., of Boston, E. C. Schafer of The Union Pacific Railroad, Frank Koval of The Chicago & North Western Railway, Robert Hancocks of the Southern Pacific Railroad, The Milwaukee Railroad, Mary Rhymer of the Chicago Historical Society, Lola Homsher of the Wyoming State Historical Department, Nora Wilson of Pullman Standard, Brown Brothers and Ewing Galloway. To all of these the author is indebted for much kindness and great courtesy of effort, research and patience. And finally he is obligated to Gerald M. Best, a repository Trismegistus of the fact and folklore of American rail transport, for reading the manuscript copy and diverting the author from numerous ways of error and directing his footsteps in the highway of veracity.

Title Page Painting by Stan Repp

Endpapers by E. S. Hammack

Published by Howell-North Books
Copyright © 1963 by Howell-North Books

Distributed in the United States by
Oak Tree Publications, Inc.
San Diego, California

Printed and bound in the United States of America.
Library of Congress Catalogue Card No. 63-22352
ISBN 0-8310-7038-2

5 6 7 8 9 85 84 83 82

We sing the wondrous story no nation sang before!
A continental chorus that echoes either shore.
We sing it on the summit; we sing it on the plain!
We've climbed the Grand Sierras
With The Lightning! The Lightning! The Lightning Palace Train!

Henry Clay Work

Contents

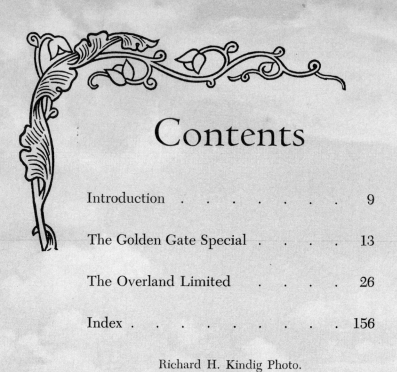

Richard H. Kindig Photo.

Cheyenne, Wyoming, 1954   Lucius Beebe

Introduction

The Overland Limited, in its mature and useful lifetime, was by no means the most distinguished, opulent or celebrated name train in the long tally of American railroad transport. The New York Central's *Twentieth Century Limited* can legitimately lay claim to greater world renown and status as an American institution. The level of voluptuousness was immeasurably more exalted on the Santa Fe's most exquisitely appointed *De Luxe* and upon the Southern Pacific's ranking candy train of all time, *The Sunset Limited* in its finest flowering at the turn of the century. Many trains from *The Congressional Limited* to the *Orange Blossom Special* and *The Chief* boasted sailing lists freighted with a greater density of famous names, a category in which *The Century* probably ranked them all. More patrician dignity rode the New Haven's *Knickerbocker* and *Merchants Limited* and greater inherited wealth on the *Bar Harbor Express.* It is probable that the cuisine on *The Panama Limited* was more supernal.

The Overland was never a "than which" train in any special field of distinction, but it had about it a style and there was a cachet of romance about its going that seems to have attached to no other name train in *The Official Guide.*

Other trains might serve vast metropolises of financial and industrial significance, traffic with resorts of more elevated social *ton* or traverse routes of superior scenic grandeur. None of them partook of the quality of being Western that was an essential characteristic of *The Overland Limited.* None of them served San Francisco, a name that has fluttered pulses in the American consciousness more than any other city in the record. San Francisco shared in the train's quality of being Western because, as Bernard De Voto has remarked, "San Francisco, stranger, is West as all hell."

For many years of its lifespan *The Overland* was held in high regard by its owning carriers. Part of this time it was an all-Pullman, extra fare transcontinental carrying the supreme distinction available to railroading of being a "limited." On its equipment Pullman lavished its most expert exercise of the carbuilder's art. Its foods, while not sumptuous in the sense that Fred Harvey food or the menus on the Baltimore & Ohio were sumptuous, were of the best. Its carding was never to partake of the urgency of speed that characterized many transcontinental trains in the later age of streamlining and it never figured in any serious accidents of mischance, let alone disasters of epic dimensions.

Everything about *The Overland* was the best without ostentation, partaking of the solid assurance of a well ordered gentlemen's club so secure in its status that the superlative was taken for granted and required no straining.

But the magic that for a full half century surrounded the name of *The Overland Limited,* derived, I think from the route it followed. Its rails led without equivocation through the illimitable spaces of what had once been the land of buffalos and Indian scouts, of the processional covered wagons and the heart's desire of the American people. The pilots of its locomotives led straight to the horizon of the farthest ocean where, if the Manitou spoke sooth, was the edge of the world over whose rim the soul must one day plunge to everlasting forgetfulness.

The mystique of American belief in The West, which has always been far stronger than religious compulsion or social creed, was, from the beginning, part of the lading of *The Overland.* It was a train of conscious emotional fulfillment.

"During the full century while it was being explored and settled, the West was for the rest of the

United States a country of strangeness and wonder, of spectacle and adventure," wrote De Voto. "Therefore it was mysterious; it was under a spell or cast a spell. It was seen through a mist of enchantment, a residue of which still exists in the minds of Easterners and Westerners alike. That residue composes the myth of the Old West, which is livelier and more widespread than the myth of the Old South ever was. (There has never been in Richmond or Charleston a store called Southern Outfitters, purveying crinolines, satin weskits and matched sets of duelling pistols to the tourist trade.) Some of the ingredients of the myth have been caused by nostalgia working on our experience in occupying the wilderness; the rest are imaginary. In our feeling about the West, fantasy and nostalgia mingle with the realities so thoroughly that few realize they are different."

In its lifespan the trafficking of *The Overland Limited* bridges the transition from mystery to factual reality, the magnitude of its scope depending upon which date one cares to accept as the veritable commencement of service, 1887 or 1899. For *The Overland Limited* was inaugurated over the Chicago & North Western and Union Pacific twelve years before its name appeared on the Southern Pacific timecard, a source of confusion to historians that will receive more extended mention herein.

If the latter date is accepted *The Overland* still had its roots in the nineteenth century, the era that had seen the emergence of the Old West upon the national consciousness and was still available in many of its conventional manifestations as late as 1905 when, at Phoenix, Arizona, an English dude was lassoed from the observation platform of the *Sunset Limited* for staring at the peasantry through a single eyeglass. If the earlier date marks the true natal year of *The Overland*, the train had its beginnings only two years after Geronimo had been lifting white scalps and three years before the Federal census of 1890 established the fact that the frontier, as it had so long been known, had finally disappeared.

Reference to photographic views of the Wyoming, Utah and Nevada communities through which *The Overland* passed as late as 1900, Julesburg, Laramie, Ogden, Corinne, Elko and Winnemucca will abundantly refute the notion that the last vestigial traces of the West of Buffalo Bill and George Armstrong Custer had yielded entirely to the derby hats, the gang plows and the smoking factories so loudly lamented by Frederick Remington.

And if *The Overland's* western terminal of San Francisco was part of the dream image of American wonderment and envy and was to continue as such until the fire and earthquake of 1906, its eastern terminal in Chicago was scarcely less conspicuous in the national consciousness as a metropolis of bounce and vitality that had already achieved its own body of folk-legend as the hog butcher to the universe and a roost of millionaires so affluent and worldly that they didn't need to tip their silk hats in the direction of Whitneys or Vanderbilts or even the godlike J. P. Morgan himself. The World's Columbian Exposition of 1893 had effectively placed Chicago on the map as a Phoenix arisen from the ashes of 1871, Mrs. Potter Palmer's diamonds and "five glass landau" and the silver dollar parquet of the barber shop in her husband's eye-popping hotel not to mention the lavish infamies of the Everleigh Club, the most luxuriously upholstered love store in the world, all were giving Chicago a reputation for worldliness and sophistication foreigners were anxious to see at first hand.

Chicago's wickedness, wealthy ways and high adrenalin content were attracting world attention and the increasing presence of foreign travelers including journalists on whom the twenty course dinners in Fifth Avenue and spurious aloofness of Newport were beginning to pall. Chicago was, quite literally, something to write home about.

The Overland Limited connected at either end of its run the two most exciting and in many ways enviable American metropolises. Between its terminals it followed the course of westering empire along the American equivalent of a pious Moslem's pilgrimage to Mecca or the Golden Journey to Samarkand. Through the pastoral beauty of summer in Iowa, along the margins of the North Platte, across the Great Plains where the Mormon handcarts had rolled into the Wells Fargo country beyond the Shining Mountains and at length through Nevada haunted by a hundred convulsive bonanzas to California the golden, was a holy journey, as devout a landfaring in the American faith as a visit to Jerusalem had been to a knight of the Crusades.

All along the route of *The Overland* were wayside shrines in the national religion of the ineffable West: at Council Bluffs Abraham Lincoln had gazed across the wide Missouri and said in effect: "Yonder runs your railroad." At Julesburg, Cheyenne and Sidney had been the jumping off places in the Black Hills gold rush of only yesterday. As the rails veered southward beyond Green River toward Echo Canyon and the Valley of the Saints they passed almost within rifle shot of Fort Bridger where the last and greatest of The Mountain Men had settled to become himself an object of veneration when he showed visitors the suit of medieval body armor presented him by Sir St. George Gore, farthest roving of the great generation of British milords who hunted the buffalo before William Cody had been invented. Along the Sink of Humboldt in Nevada they envisioned in the mind's eye the wagon tracks marked with animal carcasses, roadside graves and the cherished family possessions discarded by the overland emigrants in their last desperate effort to survive into the watershed and shadow of the High Sierra. When they reached the Sierra themselves, there were dark intimations of the melancholy Donners and beyond the Sierra was the California of every heart's desire.

Since the caravans out of India of the middle ages no landfaring inherited more implications of romance than the mainline from Lake Michigan to the Golden Gate that fell, in the fullness of time like ripened fruit, into the capable hands of Edward H. Harriman.

When, through the processes of attrition and ineptitude that seem to be the special genius of railroading in the second half of the twentieth century in the United States, *The Overland* was progressively downgraded and finally eliminated from the timecards of carriers that had once held it in such high regard, something of wonder and glory vanished from the lexicon of the Western plains. More than any other name train on the far side of the wide Missouri it has symbolized the West that had once been a preoccupation of the American people, but that had itself been overwhelmed in the tidal surge of mediocrity that passes for progress and the devaluation of people that is the inevitable consequence of their multiplication. On its cars when they first ran out of Omaha in the eighties had ridden, in their proper persons, the peace officers and Indian scouts, the cavalry commanders, shotgun messengers, route agents for Wells Fargo and satraps of the Comstock Lode that are now forever in the Valhalla of national folk-legend. *The Overland* had itself been part of the mighty pageant and continental dimension that are now no more than fakements in the property rooms of Culver City.

The Overland Limited, stabled though it may be for all time in the final coach yards beyond the marge of Acheron, is a name for American immortality, the peer in splendid implications of Union Pacific and Santa Gertrudis, of Santa Fe and the Oregon Trail, Wells Fargo, South Pass and Little Big Horn, a name to catch at the throat of national remembrance. That is why the author has been moved to write this book about a train whose name must forever be a great blaze of memory, *THE OVERLAND LIMITED*.

LUCIUS BEEBE

Virginia City, 1963.

Elko, Nevada, 1915

Fred Jukes

The Golden Gate Special

It is a notable circumstance and well established in the record that many of the most distinguished name trains in American railroad history have had, as it were, trial runs under other names before becoming permanent fixtures in the pages of *The Official Guide*. The first of the New York Central's famous fleet of twenty hour trains on the New York Chicago run of which *The Twentieth Century Limited* was to become the bright particular star was an experimental de luxe varnish haul called *The Exposition Flyer*, an all-Wagner extra fare train on a twenty hour carding which was inaugurated in 1893 to serve the World's Columbian Exposition at Chicago and which was discontinued at the end of the same year when the fair closed. The operational data deriving from this highly successful experiment was the basis for inaugurating the immortal *Century* nine years later.

In much the same manner the rival Pennsylvania in the same year and on the same twenty hour schedule tried out an all-Pullman *de luxe* train to ferry patrons in style to the Chicago Exposition called *The Pennsylvania Special* which, in the fullness of time, achieved a permanent place in the folklore of railroading as *The Broadway Limited*.

Less explicit, perhaps, is the connection between the New York & New England Railroad's now legendary "White Train" between Boston and New York in the nineties and the later and equally celebrated *Merchants Limited* of the succeeding New Haven Railroad, but the blood-lines of the Santa Fe's unbelievably opulent *De Luxe* were clearly discernible when *The Chief* came into being in the 1920s while *The Chief* itself may be regarded, in the long light of history, as an out-of-town tryout for *The Super Chief*.

The inaugural and eventual confirmation of the character of the train that became *The Overland Limited* followed a different formula, for instead of a pilot train operated as an experiment before it was placed in service, the train which was to give *The Overland* its cachet of style was actually operated on a parallel schedule after the name Overland itself first appeared on the Union Pacific timecards. *The Overland Flyer*, Trains Nos. 3 and 4, whose formal title was to be changed in 1895 to *The Overland Limited*, went into service between Council Bluffs and San Francisco on a daily schedule November 13, 1887. West of Ogden on the Central Pacific leg of the journey it was not known as *The Overland* for another twelve years, but simply lost its identity in the connecting *Pacific Express* westbound and *Atlantic Express* eastbound.

From December 5, 1888 until May 12, 1889, a curiously out-of-season time for such a venture, there was run on a parallel schedule the all-Pullman, extra fare, de luxe limited known as *The Golden Gate Special*, a name by which it was known both on the Union Pacific and Central Pacific, and a train whose overtones of luxury and special equipment were eventually to be incorporated in *The Overland*. It represented the paradox of a prototypal train placed in service after the name flyer which was to be modeled on it and operating, briefly, in competition with the train that was to absorb its dominant characteristics.

This was not the first time an all-Pullman train had been placed in service between Omaha and San Francisco. Such a run had been envisioned in the fall of 1869 barely half a year after the driving of the Gold Spike at Promontory and had obviously been designed to supplement the daily coach and Palace cars trains with a more voluptuous conveyance operating on an eighty-one hour schedule between terminals for the de luxe trade.

On October 15, 1869 display advertisements in the name of the Union Pacific Railroad announced the inaugural of *The Special Palace Car Express* between San Francisco and Omaha with all meals served on board.

A special train of Pullman Palace Hotel Drawingroom and sleeping cars will leave Omaha at 9:15 A.M. every Tuesday commencing October 19, 1869, and will run through to San Francisco without change arriving there Friday afternoon.

Returning, this special train will leave San Francisco at 7:30 A.M. every Monday commencing October 5, 1869 and arrive at Omaha Thursday afternoon, connecting with FAST ATLANTIC EXPRESS for all points east. Passengers by this train from San Francisco arrive in New York the following Sunday morning.

Fare by this special train between Omaha and San Francisco including double berth in sleeping car $168.00 currency.

Meals will be served on this train, viz: Breakfast, 7 to 9, $1.00; Lunch 11 to 2, card prices; Dinner 4 to 5, $1.50.

This train is specially designed for through passengers and will stop only at points necessary for fuel and water.

Passage tickets, drawing rooms, sections and berths, can be secured by telegram or personal application at the General Office of the Pullman Pacific Car Co., 102 Michigan Avenue, Chicago, at the office of the U. P. R. R. Omaha and at the office of the Central Pacific R. R. San Francisco.

A. N. TOWNE, *General Supt.*
CPRR Sacramento, California,

C. G. HAMMOND, *General Supt.*
UPRR Omaha,

GEO. M. PULLMAN, *President*
Pullman Pacific Car Co., Chicago.

Just how long this experimental all-Palace Car train remained in operation, in the absence of time-cards for the period, is not today known, but it may be assumed from oblique references to it in company literature twenty and more years later that it was of brief duration. Promotional pamphlets, some of them of a costly and ornate nature, issued by the Union Pacific in the nineties to advertise *The Overland Limited* speak of an Omaha to California Pullman train, but explain its abandonment on the grounds that the Palace Car equipment, then much heavier than ordinary coaches and head-end revenue cars, caused so much damage to tracks and right of way as to necessitate its withdrawal after a brief period. The speeds necessary for the eighty-one hour schedule are also mentioned as a contributing factor "roadmasters complaining that the regular scheduling of these

fast, heavy trains were reducing racks and right of way to a condition where they would soon be inoperable."

It is possible that lack of patronage was also a contributing factor, although one not likely to be mentioned in company literature. For the first few years, or at least after the curiosity and novelty had worn off, patronage was barely sufficient to warrant the continuance of the *Atlantic and Pacific Expresses* between Omaha and California on a daily basis.

The hope of a revival of special services and Palace Car traffic appears again sixteen years later in 1885 when the Chicago, Burlington & Quincy Railroad advertised a through hotel car from Chicago to the coast beginning May 12. This was to be aboard the "elegant sleeper and hotel car *Yellowstone*," that had been built the year previous by Jackson & Sharp at Wilmington for the Worcester Excursion Car Company of Massachusetts. It was to operate once a week over the Burlington to Council Bluffs where it was to be integrated to the Union Pacific's *Pacific Express* westbound and *Atlantic Express* eastbound and it apparently was the first car to run without change of passengers between Chicago and California. Through car connections via the Chicago & North Western were still, at this date, two years in the future. Aboard the *Yellowstone* "competent cooks, waiters, porters, etc., will be furnished and meals served at the rate of 75 cents each. The cost of transportation in this car will be $162.50 for each passenger and $35 per day for the service of sleeper or $2 per day each for a party of 18."

The all-Pullman experiment of 1869, brief-lived though it may have been, and the Burlington's hotel car all the way from Lake Michigan to Oakland were the pioneers pointing the way for the establishment in the fall of 1887 of regular daily service with through cars over the North Western, Union Pacific and Central Pacific in the form of *The Overland Flyer*.

Let us, in the mind's eye evoked by Shakespeare, envision "the vasty fields of France" before Harfleur, turn back the clock to contemplate the Union Pacific's depot at Omaha in the now distant year of 1888. It is a radiant summer's morning and the same train shed is serving the pioneer carrier that we see so graphically depicted in the double truck illustrations that delighted readers of *Harper's* and *Leslie's* weeklies and the other picture press of the time, a massive sooty structure with a peaked roof supported by an iron network of beams and struts where the locomotive whistles, the bells that announced the impending departure of trains, the cries of vendors of periodicals and basket lunches, the banshee screams of misplaced children and the crash of primitive couplings suggest the return of Chaos and Old Night.

This is the counterpart, on the western frontier of civilization, and in terms of its contemporary America, of the scene that so fascinated the novelists of Victorian England who delighted in the railroad depot atmosphere and personalities of London in a day of hansom carriages and brilliantly painted locomotive engines where the driver and firemen rode footplates naked to the elements without benefit of cab or cabin and before the corridor car was invented.

Many of the properties are identical and, for that matter, a ponderable part of the personnel at Omaha, for it was the heyday of the traveling English milord who was contemplating the heights of the Himalayas, the White Nile and the plains of Kansas from behind an impartially inquisitive and appraising monocle.

Except for his single eyeglass and Dundreary weepers, the English milord was practically indistinguishable from his American cousin, the well-to-do Bostonian and New Yorker intent on the heady excitements of the newly opened West and appraising, with a more calculating eye than his British counterpart, the amazement of natural resources reaching to every horizon, all of them implicit with profit from grain and grazing, mine, mill and townsite. It the the age of the silk top hat and broadcloth tailcoat even in the frontier towns and howling wilderness of California and Nevada, and of the Inverness cloak and fore-and-aft deerstalker hat affected alike by world travelers and by Sherlock Holmes of Baker Street. The quantities of luggage that accompanied the traveler upon his most simple occasions was stupifying: mounds of Saratoga trunks to tax the muscles of sweating porters, mountains of Gladstone valises that threatened the very lives, if started in avalanche, of baggagemasters, silk hat boxes, rolled steamer rugs, port-manteaux, wicker crates, lunch baskets, patent writing

desks, gun cases, fishing apparatus, sheathed telescopes, specimen boxes for flowers and butterflies, the sketching easels of artists, faggots of walking sticks and traveling book cases crammed with maps, handy hints for voyagers and *Crofutt's Guides* in endless profusion and in a multiplicity and disorder that made the services of a trained guide imperative at important terminals.

If there were a photographer present, he was apt to be a professional, for today's bandoleered amateur cameraman was in the unforeseen future, and his apparatus was of fearful proportions, a vast view camera of brass-bound mahogany wood, plate cases of formidable dimensions and a portable dark room that could, at the end of the track, be mounted on a buggy wherein to coat his glass plates with collodion solution before exposure and develop them only minutes afterward. Army officers posted to Fort Laramie or the Presidio at San Francisco clattered with sabers and map cases, professional geologists with picks and portable chemistry sets, traveling salesmen with sample cases in infinite variety. America on the move in the year 1887 was a glacial progress of portable properties.

But all this massive impedimenta is not destined for the train upon which we are about to take passage. It may well belong to the fortunate passengers holding space on *The Golden Gate Special,* but only the most essential elements of personal toilette will actually accompany them aboard its gleaming varnish, for the management in a sternly worded edict forbids all luggage in excess of 150 pounds, and the folding writing desks, geology specimens, cases of matched English shotguns with ammunition in abundance, will follow in the less exalted baggage cars of Train No. 2 *The Pacific Express.* A mere 150 pounds in the year 1887 can scarcely contain the vital necessities for overnight but it must suffice four full days of overland travel. There will be no evening dress at dinner time as on *The Blue Train* between Paris and Monte Carlo and no portable wine cellars will accompany their aristocratic owners with the vintages of '65 and '72 such as are lifted into the staterooms of the *Simplon-Orient Express,* but our passengers will make do. What they lack in personal articles of convenience and adornment, *The Golden Gate Special* will itself supply in gratifying multiplicity.

For this train is unlike any other that has to date traveled down the high iron anywhere beyond the wide Missouri and available to the general public upon payment of the cash fare, in this case a flat $100 from Omaha to the Golden Gate of its name. True, there had been the all-Pullman Boston Board of Trade train seventeen years before when the Overland Route was new and Promontory a recent memory, but that had been a private venture mounted by George M. Pullman whose publicity awareness was only matched by his genius as hotelier. Aboard it only State Street magnates and their ladies and railroad officials of flag rank had been invited to dine of canvasback duck and listen to organ recitals in the Palace Car *Palmyra*. *The Golden Gate Special* was available to all comers, either ladies or gentlemen, who had the foresight to wire ahead for reservations and could afford the tariff aforementioned, representing $60 for straight rail fare, and $40 surcharge.

There is evidence in the record to suggest that the promotional success and general réclame deriving from the all-Pullman Board of Trade train suggested to both Pullman and the Union Pacific the inaugural of a regularly scheduled luxury train, probably on a weekly basis, as far back as 1870. A single hotel car or at the most two were assigned to *The Atlantic* and *The Pacific Expresses* at that time, diners were not yet in operation at all on the Overland run, and the opinion was apparently well grounded that a weekly de luxe run could be made to pay off. George Pullman was more than willing to supply the equipment and the U.P. management was all for it, but a single factor and that a determining one, stood in the way of the project. This was the state of track and roadbed in 1870. Even the passage of a single train of all-Pullmans bearing the Boston party had caused much damage to the light iron of the time in the form of cracked rails and damaged joints and it was the unanimous opinion of roadmasters and superintendents all the way from the Missouri to Sacramento that the regular scheduling of such ponderous consists would shortly render the entire system inoperable. In the intervening years, however, greatly improved roadbeds with seventy pound rail and more sophisticated ballasting had been introduced both on the Union Pacific and the Central

Pacific. It was in reality the substantially heavier rails that made possible the innovation of all-Pullman service in the form of *The Golden Gate Special*.

It was a new adventure into the field of luxury travel, the overland counterpart of the splendid steamships Samuel Cunard had already had in trans-Atlantic service for three full decades and perhaps the first emergence of the status symbol on the Western continent. When one boarded its cars he had arrived both socially and economically just as surely as if he dined regularly among the voluptuaries who patronized Potter Palmer's hotel beside Lake Michigan or waded decorously in bathing attire that reached from neck to ankles at Bailey's Beach in primeval Newport.

That the Pullman Palace Carbuilding Company and executives of the Union Pacific had contemplated the operation of an all-Pullman train on the Overland Route for several years before the actual inaugural of the Golden Gate cannot be doubted. The manufacture of the cars that were to be included in its consist can hardly have taken less than a twelve-month period and the operational problems implicit in running and dispatching a heavy train at fifty mile an hour speeds over seventy pound rail, then the heaviest of any roadbed on the continent, must have entailed long and prayerful consideration. So, too, must the incorporation of an impressive variety of then highly experimental innovations and unprecedented luxuries which were to include electric lights activated by a steam motor connecting with the locomotive boiler to drive a dynamo in the baggage compartment, separate tub baths for ladies and gentlemen with abundant hot and cold water, a gentlemen's barber shop, the services of a valet de chambre to tend to gentlemen's attire, a matron to attend the ladies and mind the children, a cuisine of continental implications and a library car stocked with books for every taste. "The amiable, but persistent, peanut boy and news vendor" were banished in favor of a well stocked buffet and humidor while the daily papers were to be taken on at appropriate points along the line. Fresh cut flowers for the dining car, ferns for planters in the observation salon, specially monogrammed bed and table linen and richly embossed stationery were all part of the scheme of things that was to make passage on the

Golden Gate a memorable occasion and spread the fame alike of railroad and Pullman to the far corners of the earth.

When it was placed in service practically on the heels of *The Golden Gate Special* in the autumn of 1887, *The Overland Limited* was, of practical necessity, to abate some of these luxurious appointments and amenities which were not to reappear in their *tout ensemble* and with variations until the building of the first all-Pullman *Sunset Limited* for the Southern Pacific Railroad in 1895 for the run, at first, between San Francisco and Chicago via Texas and eventually between California and New Orleans as it runs today.

The Pullman Palace cars originally advertised for the *Golden Gate* were the aptly named *Golden Gate* with a baggage compartment, space for the pioneer electric light plant, barber shop and gentleman's bath; the diner *Casa Monica* for the service of three meals a day, the sleepers *Khiva* and *Rahula*, each with twelve sections, a lady's bathroom and toilets, and a drawing room for the occupancy of nabobs or valetudinarians; and the composite car *Aladdin* which comprised "six luxurious sleeping sections, a Buffet and a large open room furnished with easy chairs, a library, writing materials, and which will be used for smoking and, more particularly as an observation room. The end windows are very large, extending from the top of the car to within fifteen inches of the floor and afford a full view of the magnificent scenery en route."

There was also another, possibly stand-by observation sleeping car, the magnificent *Sybaris* which the builder's photographs show to have carried both the names of the Union and Central Pacific Railroads and *The Golden Gate Special* on its nameboards. No mention seems to be made in the company's promotional prospectuses at the time of the observation platforms which were part of the economy of both *Sybaris* and *Aladdin*, but which are believed by Arthur Dubin, ranking authority on the history of American carbuilding, to have been the first to be embodied in any Pullman-built Palace cars and, as such, forerunners of the brass railed open platform which throughout the golden age of railroad travel was to be the hallmark of a name train of prestige and pretentions.

Not only, if Mr. Dubin's surmise is correct, were *Sybaris* and *Aladdin* the prototypes of generations of brass railed observation cars yet unborn on drawing boards at Pullman and American Car & Foundry, they were probably the first of their kind anywhere between the Missouri and Great Salt Lake, at least in general service, although business and private cars such as the celebrated and beautiful *Stanford* with observation platforms at one end or both were already widely in vogue wherever the railroads ran.

West of Ogden on the Central Pacific where the Sierra crossing was one of the great American adventures of the time, flatcars fitted with benches affording an unobstructed view of the passing countryside were attached to all first class trains at Reno and Sacramento. Some, apparently were also in service on the run around the north end of Great Salt Lake although the desolate landscape of Northern Utah can have afforded little satisfaction to the most avid tourist. The Central's first observation cars were open to the elements and unroofed, but the rain of soot and live cinders from the wood burning locomotives up front proved so ruinous to well brushed silk hats and dainty crinolines that the car superintendent shortly devised roofed-over cars with open sides in their place. These improvised rolling grandstands shown in numerous photographs of the early seventies paused for 10 minutes in all trains that rounded Cape Horn in the High Sierra by daylight.

In addition to the unlisted *Sybaris* there were also two additional Pullman sleepers assigned to the Golden Gate, *Australia* and *New Zealand* whose resources of mahogany, rich draperies and ample upholstery all contained in vistas of bevel-edged French mirrors were to add to the luxurious aspect of travel on this favored train.

In an age when railroad accidents were approaching the dimensions of a national scandal and taking passage on the cars involved all the risks of disintegration that were later to be implicit in flying, the proprietors of *The Golden Gate Special* were at pains to emphasize the practical aspects of safety which had been incorporated in the train's economy and its operation. Air brakes and automatic couplers were already taken universally for granted on first class carriers, but Pullman made much of the fact that the *Golden Gate* was of vestibule construction throughout, then something of a novelty, and that "the Pullman-Sessions Patents, exclusively owned by the Pullman Company, almost entirely remove the tendency to the swaying and oscillation of cars by the use of plates at the point of contact, sustained in place by powerful springs, which produce a continuous and perfect alignment of cars — in fact a solid train."

A regular fire brigade was also organized among train employees in the event of derailment and the possible firing of the debris to which trains were subject in an age before all-steel construction rendered fire hazard negligible. "The train is supplied with the best chemical extinguishers, axes, etc., and fire hose attached to the pressure water tanks in each car, while the brigade is thoroughly drilled for fire duty."

All these amenities, conveniences and safety measures were to be taken for granted by another generation of railroad travelers. In 1887 the Gold Spike Ceremony at Promontory had been history for less than two decades and passengers on the transcontinental railroad were setting out on a voyage still adventurous over remote and uninhabited distances where well within the memory of many passengers the buffalo herds had roamed in uncounted numbers and Sioux war parties had been a factual menace to the pioneers. There was real and tangible romance in the occupancy of a splendid Palace Car, steam heated and electrically illuminated, to be seated at table with irreproachable linen and service for choice viandes and vintage wines where only forty years ago the covered wagons had drawn into a protective circle for the night's camp and a wagon bed was the most luxurious couch within a thousand miles.

Taking the cars out of Omaha for California involved almost precisely the same passage of time as is required today for ocean travel between New York and Southampton, and, once headed west along the margins of the North Platte, the trains were almost as self contained and without recourse to outside assistance as an ocean liner in the days before Marconi. The Pullmans of *The Golden Gate Special* were a microcosm of luxury and convenience functioning in an almost lifeless void of plains and desert, sky and mountains, where fuel for the locomotives and water for the cars were almost the only resources of operational stops. A water tank tended by a whiskered ancient in the Nevada wasteland was like the sight of a passing

vessel at sea, the meet with a train bound in the opposing direction a major event of the day.

On the inaugural of the *Golden Gate*, the train's proprietors lavished the most urbane and enticing promotion known to a pre-Madison Avenue age. Travel agents everywhere, functionaries then endowed with no small importance as proconsuls of the carriers and able to route unknowing patrons over any line that enjoyed their favor, were alerted to its almost unearthly appointments and the exalted status of the clientele the management solicited. Handsome brochures were confected with expertly executed steel engravings and appropriate letterpress and run on creamy stock by Rand McNally & Co., of Chicago, who were then the universal printers to the railroad trade. A special typescript, reproduced in this volume, in ornate Spencerian was devised as the identifying hallmark of the *Golden Gate* and the slogan "The Finest Train in The World" was incorporated in all timetables, schedules, advertising and promotional matter much as, only a few years later, Rolls Royce was to characterize its product as "The Finest Car in The World."

It is only a pity that a guest book was not kept of the fortunate voyagers who took passage aboard the cars of the *Golden Gate*, but the practice, alas, did not come into vogue until the maintenance of a daily sailing list became part of the operational procedure of *The Twentieth Century Limited* a decade and a half in the future. What great names boarded the noble cars *Khiva* and *Rahula* and smoked their Havannah Puros in the buffet of *Aladdin* must be left to conjecture, but it may be imagined they were exalted beyond the ordinary, for *The Golden Gate Special* was no ordinary train. As Cole Porter was to pronounce it in verse and music, "Fancy things are for the fancy folk," and no fancier artifact rode the rails in the United States than the train that whistled off from Omaha in December of 1888 with the barber standing at attention in *Golden Gate* and the maitre d'hotel in his white linen waistcoat of office putting final touches on the place services laid for first luncheon on *Casa Monica*.

The Golden Gate Special left Council Bluffs at eight in the morning and cleared the U. P. depot at Omaha fifteen minutes later, arriving at San Francisco at nine-thirty the evening of the third day out. This, taking into consideration the Chicago & North Western, the Burlington or Rock Island connection with Chicago to account for the better part of another day and overnight run to make the early morning departure of the *Golden Gate* placed San Francisco four traveling days from the Great Lakes or five from New York.

The management was, as has been suggested above, very strict in the matter of luggage. "Under no circumstances will excess baggage be checked for this train," read the timetable. "Baggage not to exceed 150 pounds for each full fare and 75 pounds for each half ticket will be carried free. All baggage in excess of this amount will be forwarded on the regular train following (in this case *The Overland Flyer*). No baggage will be checked through for this train. Owners must claim baggage and have it rechecked at Council Bluffs Transfer."

Equally firm was the Union Pacific in the matter of reserved space.

"As accommodations on this train are limited, early application should be made, and the accommodation thus secured paid for at once on arrival from the East at Council Bluffs," it announced. "Reservations not paid for thirty minutes before train leaves will be cancelled and disposed of to other applicants."

Whether the firm tone of this admonition was in fact justified by the press of patronage cannot, at this remove, be ascertained. Certainly the proprietors of the first of all de luxe flyers in the Old West felt that they had achieved sufficient reward in the form of publicity and prestige from their investment. Certainly, too, they were convinced that, with certain modifications in the sumptuousness of its overall operation, a first class luxury run via the Overland Route was justified, not as a once a week novelty, but on a daily basis. For, brief as had been the lifespan of the truly regal *Golden Gate*, it had no sooner disappeared from the timecard than its basic character was to be reborn, incorporated in *The Overland Flyer* which, in the course of time, was to be *The Overland Limited* which is the subject of this monograph.

THE GOLDEN GATE SPECIAL

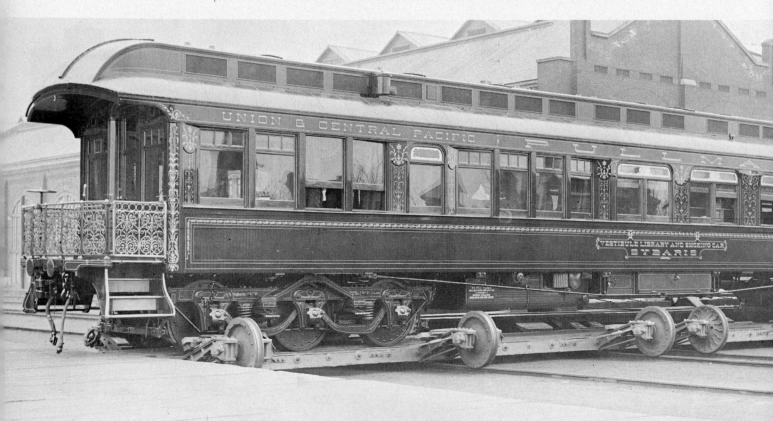

Electric lights of *The Golden Gate Special* were activated by power plant in baggage compartment shown opposite. Observation lounge *Aladdin* and sleeper *Australia*, shown here, were last word in voluptuous travel as was the barber shop for gentlemen. *(Photos: Pullman Standard; Line Drawings: Southern Pacific.)*

page 21

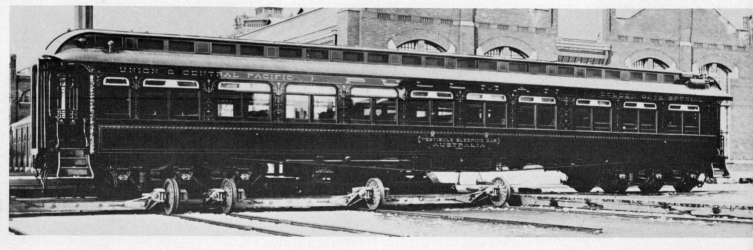

The Golden Gate Special.

The Golden Gate Special.	Miles.	STATIONS.	Miles.	The Golden Gate Special.
.00 A.M	0	Lv...COUNCIL BLUFFS ..Ar.	1867	9.00 A.M
.15 "	3	" ....OMAHA.......... "	1864	8.45 "
.00 P.M	156	" ....GRAND ISLAND.... "	1711	4.20 "
.10 "	294	" ....NORTH PLATTE.... "	1573	12.35 "
.40 "	417	" ....SIDNEY......... "	1450	8.20 P.M
.45 "	519	" ....CHEYENNE....... "	1348	5.35 "
.10 A.M	576	" ....LARAMIE ..... "	1291	3.10 "
.30 "	712	" ....RAWLINS........ "	1155	10.50 A.M
.55 "	848	" .....GREEN RIVER..... "	1019	6.25 "
.15 P.M	958	" ....EVANSTON....... "	909	3.05 "
45 "	1034	" ....OGDEN .... "	833	12.15 "
.45 "	1253	" ....WELLS.......... "	614	3.45 P.M
.30 A.M	1333	" .....CARLIN .... "	534	1.00 "
....	1342	" ....PALISADE....... "	525	....
.15 "	1453	" .....WINNEMUCCA..... "	414	9.00 A.M
.40 "	1589	" ..... WADSWORTH..... "	278	4.50 "
.50 "	1623	" ....RENO.......... "	244	3.20 "
.30 "	1658	" ....TRUCKEE........ "	209	2.00 "
.40 P.M	1723	" ....COLFAX .... "	144	9.15 P.M
.15 "	1777	" .....SACRAMENTO..... "	90	5.50 "
.45 P.M	1867	Ar....SAN FRANCISCO....Lv	0	2.00 P.M

—THIS IS—
THE FINEST TRAIN IN THE WORLD.

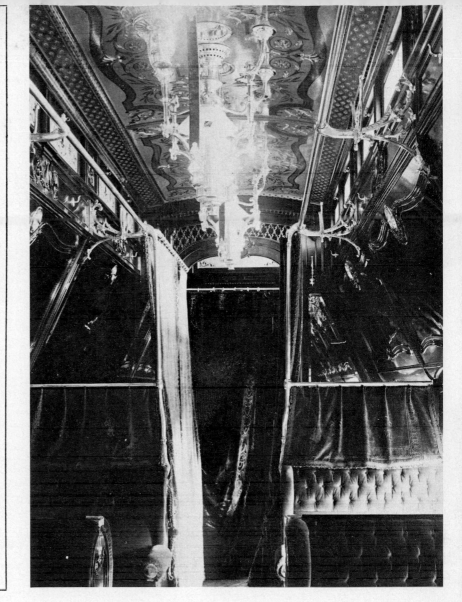

Although *The Golden Gate Special* was withdrawn from service after a single season for reasons not available in the record, it gave overland travel a foretaste of the de luxe varnish trains which were shortly to be placed in service not only on the Union Pacific-Central Pacific connection out of Omaha, but on the rival Santa Fe and on the Southern Pacific's own choicely regarded Sunset Route to Chicago and New Orleans. *The Golden Gate's* equipment included *Sybaris* and *Golden Gate*, elements of which have been depicted on previous pages, and the sleepers *Khiva* and *Rahula* and the sumptuous dining car *Casa Monica*. Arthur D. Dubin, ranking historian of the carbuilders' *expertise*, believes the open observation platforms of *Aladdin* and *Sybaris* were the first Pullman cars of this design. In addition to the equipment listed, there were standby sleepers *Australia* (shown opposite), *New Zealand* and *China*, the last of which is shown above in an interior view. "As accommodations on this train are limited early application should be made and accommodations paid for at once on arrival from the east at Council Bluffs," said the company's promotional literature sternly. "Reservations not paid for thirty minutes before the train leaves will be canceled and disposed of to other applicants." The tariff for services on *The Golden Gate Special* was two bits for a shave, a half dollar for haircut or shampoo and seventy-five cents for a bath. *(All Pictures: Arthur D. Dubin Collection.)*

Although well within the era of the photographic record, no wet plate likeness of *The Golden Gate Special* has been turned up to date and the only image of the entire train is the fanciful line drawing reproduced below from the elaborate brochure published by the passenger department of Union Pacific in 1888. The records of the Pullman Company, however, preserved both interiors and exteriors of its fabulous Palace equipment and they are shown in the pages devoted to this train. Above is the artist's version of the ladies' bathroom and the diner set up for the service of luncheon. *(Photos: Pullman Standard; Line Drawings: Southern Pacific.)*

The Golden Gate's separate baths for ladies and gentlemen, the latter shown above and at the right, sumptuous berths and well appointed buffet *(below, right)* and other amenities of luxury justified its extra fare and spread its fame as the first regularly scheduled all-Pullman flyer west of Chicago.

The Overland Limited

In the autumn of 1887 four major trunk lines connecting with Chicago and the East converged upon the complicated network of rails that made Council Bluffs, Iowa, the principal crossroads of rail traffic at that date west of Lake Michigan. They were the Chicago & North Western, the Chicago, Burlington & Quincy, the Chicago, Milwaukee & St. Paul and the Chicago, Rock Island & Pacific.

Until this year all passengers headed for points west of the Missouri via the Union Pacific had changed cars at what was known as "U. P. Transfer" at Council Bluffs. In volume of passenger traffic the North Western was easily the leader with the Burlington and the Milwaukee in that order of popularity. The Rock Island was an also-ran.

Occasional through cars had been interchanged such as the Burlington's specially scheduled *Yellowstone* mentioned in the portion of this monograph devoted to *The Golden Gate Special,* but the time was not yet when a passenger might occupy sleeping car space from Chicago all the way to California on a regularly scheduled train without changing cars at the east bank of the Missouri.

A few special trains, notably the all-Pullman luxury consist which carried members of the Boston Board of Trade to San Francisco in 1870, had been scheduled intact on a transcontinental routing, but the vast majority of passengers, until 1887, had descended from the cars of their chosen carriers and made the transition at U. P. Transfer. Railroad travelers everywhere were accustomed, if not reconciled to changing cars at terminal points, although by the date which is our concern here through accommodations between the major cities of the East and South were well established, perhaps the longest of which in point of mileage being through service from New York to New Orleans. Many a seasoned traveler well remembered when it had been obligatory to make four changes of cars between New York and Chicago and when passage between such comparatively adjacent points as Boston and New York had been available by a bewildering succession of changes from train to steamer and back to train again to achieve terminals only a little more than 200 miles apart.

Now, however, it was possible to go all the way from Chicago to Oakland aboard the de luxe accommodations of the North Western, the Union Pacific and the Central Pacific. Even the legendary change of cars from the U. P. to the C. P. at Promontory that had been obligatory at Promontory in the first years after the completion of the Pacific Railroad was now shrouded in the mists of antiquity.

The closing years of the eighties saw, too, another revolutionary step in the technique of passenger train operations and their promotion and advertising.

Nobody hitherto had stayed awake nights thinking up glamorous and romantic names for trains. To designate a train as *The Cannonball* or the *Fast Mail* in addition to their identifying numbers was considered by many general managers a concession to pure poetry. Since the Golden Spike ceremony at Promontory in 1869 the through connection from San Francisco to Council Bluffs had been known as *The Atlantic Express* eastbound and, logically enough, *The Pacific Express* westbound. Good functional working names which indicated where the cars were headed and didn't leave the management open to any suspicion of frivolity.

Now, however the trains themselves were becoming so splendid as to justify something more fanciful than the *Sacramento-Redding Passenger* or the *Los Angeles Night Train.* Silk hatted general managers stroked their long weeper whiskers and began exploring the realms of mythology, ornithology and regional folklore for designations with which to capture the fancy of travelers and insure their patronage. The days of all-Pullman extra fare flyers were at hand. Long haul runs were beginning to incorporate valets, lady's maids and barbers in their operations. Menus and wine cards were approaching the dimensions of those of Delmonico's in New York and Potter Palmer's sensational new hotel in Chicago. Already the parlor organ of the Pullman Palace Car *Palmyra* on the San Francisco run from Omaha had attracted world wide attention as a symbol of almost Babylonish luxury, and clever George Mortimer Pullman was building sleeping cars for long runs with bathtubs for hot and cold water. Everything was becoming increasingly elegant and more genteel, the two favorite words of the age, and it might be wise to dream up some elegant and genteel names for the varnish cars that were the carriers' proudest possessions.

As of November 13, 1887 the management of the Union Pacific planned to operate a fine new train, Nos. 3 and 4 west from Council Bluffs-Omaha and it wanted a name in keeping with the exalted status of its equipment and one which would catch the popular fancy as well. Something with Western overtones and regional connotations seemed indicated.

When, in the mid-sixties Bret Harte, intent on founding a magazine that should be the mirror of California's personality and a repository for the best of its lively contemporary letters, was casting about for a name that should catch the public fancy and reflect the temper of the times he came up with the name *The Overland Monthly*.

The choice was inspired and at the same time prophetic, for its connotations were the theme of everybody's wishful thinking and it had about it a ring as bright and new as the gold double eagles that were now pouring from the United States Mint at San Francisco. Harte's inspiration reached dizzying heights when he selected as the insigne or logotype of *The Monthly*, a railroad track reaching into the illimitable vistas of the future in the center of which an enormous grizzly bear was disputing the progress of an onrushing locomotive. The Central Pacific Railroad was still the incompleted dream of the men who had undertaken its construction, but Harte had sensed the wave of the future and incorporated its significance in his own editorial venture.

The bear and the railroad combined the present and the past with nice impartiality. The bear was the symbol of California's independence, the image that had appeared on the first proud flag of the short lived republic that had been so easily wrested from the hands of indifferent Spaniards, although to hear Californians tell it, the accomplishment had been a valorous undertaking and mighty military struggle. Californians admired the bear enormously and all that he stood for in courage, ferocity and cunning. They were also railroad crazy. The completing of the great Pacific railroad was in the thoughts of all men, a transcendent aspiration even then going forward in California's own Sierra in the face of seemingly insurmountable vicissitudes.

The name Overland itself was freighted with significance to Californians. It had already appeared in corporate nomenclature when *The Monthly* was born. There had been, in 1858, the Great Southern Overland Mail Route between St. Louis and California started by John Butterfield, one of the powerful old kings of hurry and express magnate whose only peer in getting the mail and passengers across the continent was equally horny handed Ben Holladay. There had also been the rival staging firm of Russell, Majors & Waddell, The Great Central Overland, California & Pike's Peak Express, and there had been the Wells Fargo-dominated Overland Mail Company which was the formal name of the immortal Pony Express. There was also the Overland Telegraph Company which shortly put the Pony Express out of business, and when he gained control of the Great Central Overland & Pike's Peak, Ben Holladay had quickly shortened it to "The Overland Stage Line" which appeared handsomely engrossed in red letters shaded with gold and maroon on the name boards of his innumerable plunging Concord coaches and lumbering express wagons.

The name Overland was worth its weight in gold in the California fifties and sixties, and it is difficult to see, as we presently shall, how the builders and eventual owners of the Central Pacific Railroad could have failed to latch onto it as an invaluable asset to their property. The record shows they not only rejected it, but went to great lengths and for many years to keep it from becoming associated with any of their operations.

But if the Big Four were insensible to the appeal of regional legend and the even then growing cult of the Old West, the managers of the Union Pacific at Omaha were not. When it set out on its maiden voyage across the Great Plains and its opposite number headed up Weber Canyon out of Ogden on November 13, 1887, the new train bore the proud name of *Overland Flyer*. It was the time when Flyers were just coming into vogue and the limited train was still in the unforseen future. Eight years later, on November 17, 1895 and conforming to the new trend, it emerged as *The Overland Limited*, a name that was destined to make railroad history for decades to come.

The Overland from the beginning carried through cars for San Francisco over the Central Pacific connection at Ogden, as well as Portland and Los Angeles sleepers, but for twelve long years after its inaugural on the Union Pacific the train's name abruptly vanished at the edge of Great Salt Lake. The Central Pacific wanted nothing of it. Its cars were integrated at Ogden to the long established *Atlantic* and *Pacific Expresses* and passengers went through in a complete continuity of passage, but not the word *Overland*. Its loss of identity the moment it got its highball out of Ogden westbound and its reassumption of that identity as soon as a U. P. locomotive was coupled to its drawbar eastbound is one of the enigmas of railroad history.

Not only did the Central Pacific, for twelve years, want nothing of *The Overland Flyer* and later *The Overland Limited*, it never acknowledged the existence of the Overland Route. Until 1899 when the long shadow of Edward Henry Harriman was already falling over the decaying empire of the Big Four, its mainline between California and Utah was designated on all Central Pacific and Southern Pacific company literature as "The Ogden Gateway Route" or in bursts of pure poetry as "The Dining Car Route."

The Big Four of the Central Pacific were as hard headed, competent and ruthless as any of the major speculative entrepreneurs of their time which is saying a great deal. They built a railroad across the North American continent on a shoestring and eventually achieved the status of truly rich millionaires in a generation when this was the crowning American achievement and article of national faith. But they had only the most primitive understanding of what we have come to call communications. Publicity and promotion were simply beyond their comprehension. If their affairs required a favorable press they bought it for cash on the barrelhead just as they bought governors and state legislatures and the favors of the government at Washington. If they couldn't buy a newspaper they suffered its calumny and abuse with the stoicism they suffered the elements. They had no conception of gentling or tempering public attitudes. If they had possessed a publicity department of even mediocre attainments it would not have been a full three decades after the Gold Spike Ceremony at Promontory before the effulgent word Overland was permitted to appear in any Southern Pacific company literature or achieve a place in its corporate lexicon.

In retrospect it is one of the most amazing facts in the history of a railroad whose affairs from any aspect they may be regarded have for almost a century been in themselves a constant amazement.

In the fullness of time the name of *The Overland Limited* was to become, with the single exception of its eastern counterpart *The 20th Century Limited*, the most radiant and celebrated train name in America. Its parent company acknowledged it as the flagship of an incomparable fleet of meticulously maintained varnish trains. New equipment and motive power were lavished upon it as jewels might be lavished on the mistress of an oriental potentate. It bore the magic numbers 1 and 2 on the operating traincards. Saloons, hotels and a brand of cigar bore its name in explicit recognition of its commercial value and to ride *The Overland Limited* on one's occasions of business or pleasure was a status symbol decades before the phrase was coined in the spurious currency of Madison Avenue.

But if the Central Pacific hierarchy from its feudal stronghold at the corner of Fourth and Townsend in San Francisco rejected all references to anything with the name Overland, it early and easily became part of the regional vocabulary of the California man in the street and the San Francisco newspapers.

When the bitter and frustrated Ambrose Bierce, as a member of the staff of the *San Francisco Ex-*

aminer in the early nineties, was devoting much of his acid talent to disemboweling the Southern Pacific, a characteristic lead to one of his stories read: "*The Overland* arrived at midnight last night, more than nine hours late."

One of the earliest of all cinema films purportedly shot in the Sierra in 1893 and depicting a Central Pacific passenger train double-heading through a characteristic cut on "The Hill" is specifically identified as "The Overland Train in California." The name crops up in common usage everywhere in the nineties despite its conspicuous absence in company literature. It was, in fact, a California institution from its inception.

East of Omaha on the Chicago & North Western, there was some initial difficulty about the new train's name, although not the determined intransigence encountered on the Central Pacific. As late as 1891 the North Western in its list of sleeping car trains in *The Official Guide* was designating its westbound section *The Overland Express*. There was also *The Pacific Limited*, daily, solid vestibule train with through Palace Car sleepers for San Francisco, Denver and Portland, no extra fare. Eastbound on the North Western chaos reigned at this period in the matter of train names. There was both an *Overland Express* and an *Overland Flyer*, the latter carrying the through varnish equipment of the train of the same name on the U. P. West of its territory, Union Pacific couldn't get its finest train name accepted at all; east of Omaha it was so much admired that two distinct trains eastbound and one westbound bore the magic name Overland. Only one of them was *The Overland Flyer*.

By 1895 when the name was officially changed to *The Overland Limited* the North Western resolved most of the confusion by conforming to the name of the U. P.'s choice.

The year 1899 was marked with a star in the annals of the Espee. A long deferred and extremely complex reorganization of the railroad's finances was accomplished that year by the terms of which a refinanced Central Pacific Railway completely owned by the Southern Pacific Company found itself in a position to inaugurate many improvements in the physical structure and operations of the railroad that had been in abeyance since the death of Leland Stanford six years earlier.

An entire overall survey of the road's Nevada lines was undertaken with an idea to effecting improvements and economies on an impressive scale. Many curves were eliminated, hundreds of miles of roadbed were reballasted, and the Lucin Cut-off across the northern end of Great Salt Lake was actively advocated by company engineers. The truth was that Edward Henry Harriman, already in control of the Union Pacific, threw a long shadow across railroading everywhere west of the Missouri River. In 1900 Collis Huntington, last of the Big Four died, and a large block of Southern Pacific securities which his family at once placed on the market turned up in the U. P. vaults at Omaha and its banks in New York. Subsequent purchases vested complete control of the Overland Rails from Omaha to San Francisco in the hands of the Little Giant of Wall Street not to mention a vast network of connecting transport in the Northwest and rail and water carriers wherever the writ of the Southern Pacific ran.

An astute student of railroading might have seen straws in the wind that indicated that the Espee's great General Manager Julius Kruttschnitt was well aware of an impending change of ownership and anxious to get the Southern Pacific in a condition that would reflect credit on his stewardship.

One of the portents of things to come appeared in *Sunset Magazine*, the Southern Pacific's court circular and official spokesman, in the issue of September 1899 reading:

> An unusually large Pacific Coast passenger traffic is expected by the transcontinental railways for the season 1899-1900, and extensive preparations are being made to care for it. There are already eight daily lines of through sleeping cars operating over the Sunset, Ogden and Shasta Routes and nine weekly or semi-weekly lines in addition. Others will be added as the season advances, and it is rumored that a sensation will be created among travelers when some of the progressive plans for comprehensive transcontinental train service become known.

In the next issue of *Sunset*, that for October which went on the newsstands early in the month, this cryptic foretaste of great events was made even more specific although the names of *The Overland Limited* and *The Shasta Limited* were not revealed.

> One of the developments consequent on the remarkable increase in transcontinental travel and

the phenomenal tourist travel to California during the coming winter, which now seems assured, is the addition of two new through trains by the Southern Pacific Company.

The new train on the Ogden Route will shorten the transcontinental time very materially. It is expected that, eastbound, about 12 hours will be lopped from the best time made by trains now running, and westbound, about 4 hours will be presented gratis to travelers by the new train.

Simultaneously with the inauguration of this new service an extra train between San Francisco and Portland will be put on, leaving northbound in the morning and arriving southbound at San Francisco in the evening. Exact schedules and full details of equipment will be announced soon.

We want to whisper in your ear that the additional train via Southern Pacific Company's Ogden Route through without change between San Francisco and Chicago will be a *gem*. Vestibuled and composed of finest equipment made, it will parallel any transcontinental train in regular service, and, by the way, the time will be shrunk about twelve hours eastbound and about four hours westbound over the existing schedules. Keep this in mind and remember that you can confidently promise your patrons the *ne plus ultra* of service if you ticket them by this train.

On October 15, 1899 *The Overland Limited* commenced operations between San Francisco and Chicago under the name it had already been known by only as far west as Ogden for the past twelve years.

In its November columns, *Sunset* for the first time in the record of Southern Pacific Company literature openly acknowledged the hitherto forbidden word "Overland," and exhorted passenger agents everywhere to sit up and pay attention to something new and splendid on the California haul.

We told you last month that the new vestibuled *Overland Limited* between San Francisco and Chicago via the Ogden Route of the Southern Pacific Company would be a gem. Well, it is! Its success has been wonderful — but then, why not? It's an Aladdin's Carpet — three days and nights between San Francisco and Chicago; all the comforts that a comfortable mind can suggest; and all the traveling luxuries a luxurious imagination knows.

Although when *The Overland* commenced its through run from Chicago to San Francisco as an acknowledged and, indeed, choicely regarded property of the Southern Pacific as well as the originating Union Pacific, it completed its transcontinental

trip between Omaha and Chicago over the left hand rails of the Chicago & North Western as it had done since 1887, this arrangement was not permanent.

For a period lasting, as far as can be ascertained, from 1905 to 1907 it made its entry to Chicago as Trains Nos. 1 and 2, *The Overland Limited* of the Chicago, Milwaukee & St. Paul Railway. The Milwaukee's passenger timetable for August 1905 lists it as part of its double daily service to Colorado, California and North Pacific Coast points, sharing billing with Train No. 3 *The California Express* and Train No. 6, *The Eastern Express*, both of which, although of secondary status, included Denver sleepers as did *The Overland*. This was in addition to the Denver car arriving in Chicago via the Rock Island which had been cut out of *The Overland* at Ogden and crossed the Rockies on the rails of the Rio Grande.

The Milwaukee's billing of *The Overland* listed a chair car and Pullman sleeper from Chicago to Denver, "one night service," a composite observation car, diner and coaches from Chicago to Omaha, a buffet-library car and diner to Denver, a standard sleeper (presumably on occasion *Glenview* and *Dakota* with the Milwaukee initials on their nameboards) Chicago to San Francisco connecting at Port Costa or Sacramento with standard sleepers for Los Angeles and at San Francisco with a buffet-sleeper train via the Coast Line to Los Angeles. An observation car and buffet-library were part of the U. P.-Espee consist west of Omaha and first class passengers changed at Green River to Pullmans and buffet-library car train to Portland. Second class passengers changed at Omaha to Union Pacific Train No. 9 which picked up a tourist sleeper at Cheyenne for Portland.

The same procedure obtained in reverse on No. 2, *The Overland* eastbound. The secondary *California Express* supplemented this service with a Salt Lake City sleeper and tourist sleepers to Los Angeles every Monday via Tracy and Fresno on the Southern Pacific. Both first class and tourist ticket holders for Butte, Helena and Portland, changed cars at Omaha.

A baffling aspect of *The Overland's* diversion or, if you will, apostacy to the Milwaukee during the years 1905 and 1906 was that during this period it still ran a section between Omaha and Chicago over the Chicago & North Western and never disappeared from the North Western's timetable of these years. Whether this was a result of an effort on the part of the Union Pacific to split its business between two connecting carriers or, as seems equally likely, a temporary feint to secure more advantageous relations with the North Western is not available to solution at this remove.

The North Western's *Overland* during this interim was strictly Pullman as indeed it was over its entire run to California over its two connecting roads, while the Milwaukee's management advertised coach accommodations on their leg of the haul and ran both Pullmans and chair cars as far as Omaha where, presumably, the chair cars terminated their run and the Pullmans were incorporated, along with the North Western's sleeping cars to make up the Union Pacific train west out of the Nebraska terminal.

It is notable that the Milwaukee's *Overland*, westbound, arrived in Omaha two hours ahead of the North Western's section, giving passengers ample time to descend from the cars although the hour, 7:35 in the morning, was not auspicious for the transaction of business. Both carriers were evidently in competition for coach business west of Chicago as is evidenced by the inaugural, in January 1906, by the North Western-Union Pacific of *The Los Angeles Limited* which carried both chair cars and Pullman accommodations to Southern California.

In any event, by 1907 *The Overland* had disappeared from the Milwaukee's timecard not to reappear there as a scheduled operation until the great switch of its transcontinental trains by the U. P. in the fifties.

Although it is no concern of this monograph, the Milwaukee in connection with the Union Pacific operated a "one night" Denver-Chicago run known as *The Chicago Special*. It is cited here to suggest the operational good terms existing between the U. P. and the Milwaukee at this time.

As late as 1906 the Milwaukee was advertising its partnership in *The Overland* in a magazine advertisement reproduced at an appropriate place in this book and stressing "the handsome new composite-observation cars, acknowledged to be the most beautiful ever placed in regular service."

The North Western's 1907 scheduling of No. 1 and No. 2 includes several interesting but hardly basic changes from the conduct of the train as a Milwaukee operation out of Chicago. Most important of these was the elevation of its status to the rank of all-Pullman "with superb Pullman Standard Drawing Room and Private Compartment sleeping cars (electric reading light in each section and compartment) and Composite-Observation Cars, with buffet and library, Chicago to San Francisco." To make a Southern California connection a train from Sacramento connected at Tracy with the Southern Pacific's *Owl* for Los Angeles and with *The Coaster* for the daylight run on the Coast Route. There were Standard Pullman sleepers between Chicago and Portland and the train briefly picked up a Pullman drawing room sleeper from Cheyenne to Ogden on the Denver-Salt Lake City run. Trains Nos. 7 and 8, the *Los Angeles Limited* on the through run from Chicago were by now in service over the San Pedro, Los Angeles & Salt Lake Railroad so the connections at Tracy and San Francisco were largely for the convenience of passengers boarding the cars in Nevada and Northern California.

From the beginning, *The Overland* carried a through car for Chicago via the Rio Grande Western from Ogden to Grand Junction, the Denver & Rio Grande from there to Denver, and the Rock Island from Denver to Chicago. The car was cut out of *The Overland* at 12:45 P.M. eastbound, left Ogden on RGW No. 2 at 2:15 P.M. and arrived in Denver the next afternoon at 3:40 P.M. It had a six hour layover in Denver, left there at 9:30 and into Chicago the second morning following at 7:59 A.M. Westbound, you left Chicago at 10 P.M. on the Rock Island, left Denver at 9:30 A.M. the second morning following, arrived in Ogden the next day on RGW No. 1 at 2 P.M. The car was cut into *The Overland* which left at 1:45 P.M. Pacific time. This went on with very little change through 1910, except in matters of minutes of arrival and leaving time. In 1910 the train left San Francisco at 10:40 A.M., arrived in Ogden at 2:10 P.M., the through car left Ogden on D&RG No. 2 at 2:55 P.M. and a slower time on the Rio Grande, arriving in Denver at 7:45 P.M. the next day, leaving at 10 P.M. on the Rock Island and into Chicago at 7:25 A.M.

California

OVERLAND LIMITED

ON THE

Chicago, Milwaukee & St. Paul Railway

IT is truly the unfolding of Nature's Wonderbook to pass through California —that land where glorious climate and rare scenic beauty hold every visitor under a spell of enchantment. This is the time to go; this is the way — The

OVERLAND LIMITED

ON THE

Chicago, Milwaukee & St. Paul Railway

The handsome new composite-observation cars are acknowledged to be the most beautiful ever placed in regular service. Sleeping and dining service so efficient and complete that there is nothing to be desired. Electric lighting throughout.

The Overland Limited leaves **Union Passenger Station,** Chicago, 8 P. M., daily. Tourist Sleepers at 10.25 P. M. Secure free literature by addressing:

F. A. MILLER
General Passenger Agent
Chicago

or

W. S. HOWELL
General Eastern Agent
381 Broadway, New York City, N. Y.

For a period of indeterminate length beginning in 1905, *The Overland* ran between Chicago and Omaha, not only over the rails of the North Western, but also on the Milwaukee in direct competition with the Vanderbilt road as did the *Pacific Limited* for many years. Its Milwaukee origins at Chicago are amply attested by the contemporary magazine advertisement on this page and the timetable opposite. At the top opposite *The Overland* is shown on the Milwaukee somewhere west of Chicago. In the early years the train insigne was on the cartop instead of in the later drumhead version on the observation car rail. But from whichever Chicago depot they departed, travelers took the Parmalee Omnibus (*left*) to and from their hotel. (*Left, Top: Arthur D. Dubin Collection; Below: Chicago Historical Society; Opposite, Top: Wyoming State Historical Department; Below: A. W. Johnson Collection.*)

THE OVERLAND LIMITED TO CALIFORNIA

VIA THE
Chicago, Milwaukee & St. Paul and Union Pacific Line
═══DOUBLE DAILY SERVICE═══
TO COLORADO AND CALIFORNIA AND NORTH PACIFIC COAST POINTS

No. 1—The Overland Limited, Electric Lighted.

Table 115	P M							
Lv Chicago	6.05	Sun	Mon	Tue	Wed	Thu	Fri	Sat
Ar { Omaha	7.35	Mon	Tue	Wed	Thu	Fri	Sat	Sun
Lv { Omaha	7.45	"	"	"	"	"	"	"
Ar Denver	9.30	"	"	"	"	"	"	"
Lv Omaha	9.40	"	"	"	"	"	"	"
Ar North Platte	5.20	"	"	"	"	"	"	"
" Cheyenne	11.00	"	"	"	"	"	"	"
" Green River	9 10	Tue	Wed	Thu	Fri	Sat	Sun	Mon
" Ogden	3.30	"	"	"	"	"	"	"
" Salt Lake City	4.45	"	"	"	"	"	"	"
" Los Angeles (via S.P.L.A.&S.L.)	7.00	Thu	Fri	Sat	Sun	Mon	Tue	Wed
" Sacramento	2.10	Wed	Thu	Fri	Sat	Sun	Mon	Tue
" San Francisco	5.48	"	"	"	"	"	"	"
Ar Los Angeles	8.55	Thu	Fri	Sat	Sun	Mon	Tue	Wed
Lv Omaha	9.40	Mon	Tue	Wed	Thu	Fri	Sat	Sun
Ar Green River	9.10	Tue	Wed	Thu	Fri	Sat	Sun	Mon
" Baker City	4.00	Wed	Thu	Fri	Sat	Sun	Mon	Tue
" Spokane	7.25	"	"	"	"	"	"	"
" Portland	5.25	"	"	"	"	"	"	"
" Tacoma	5.20	Thu	Fri	Sat	Sun	Mon	Tue	Wed
Ar Seattle	7.15	"	"	"	"	"	"	"
	A M							

The Overland Limited, Electric Lighted Throughout—One night Chicago to Denver. Standard sleeper and chair car Chicago to Denver. Composite-observation car, dining car and coaches Chicago to Omaha. Buffet-library car and dining car Omaha to Denver. Standard sleeper Chicago to San Francisco, connecting at Port Costa or Sacramento with standard sleepers for Los Angeles, and at San Francisco with buffet sleeper for Los Angeles via Coast Line. Observation car and buffet-library car Omaha to San Francisco. First-class passengers for Portland and North Pacific Coast points transfer at Green River to standard sleepers and buffet-library car. Passengers with second-class tickets for Portland transfer at Omaha to Union Pacific Train No. 9, leaving at 8.50 a. m., which train carries chair car Omaha to Cheyenne. Tourist sleeper and chair car Cheyenne to Portland. All meals in dining cars.

No. 2—The Overland Limited, Electric Lighted.

Table 117	A M							
Lv San Francisco	11.00	Sun	Mon	Tue	Wed	Thu	Fri	Sat
" Los Angeles	5.00	Sat	Sun	Mon	Tue	Wed	Thu	Fri
" Sacramento	2.20	Sun	Mon	Tue	Wed	Thu	Fri	Sat
" Los Angeles (via S.P.L.A.&S.L.)	7.30	Sat	Sun	Mon	Tue	Wed	Thu	Fri
" Salt Lake City	1.40	Mon	Tue	Wed	Thu	Fri	Sat	Sun
" Ogden	3.00	"	"	"	"	"	"	"
" Green River	9.20	"	"	"	"	"	"	"
" Cheyenne	7.03	Tue	Wed	Thu	Fri	Sat	Sun	Mon
" North Platte	1.08	"	"	"	"	"	"	"
Ar } Omaha	8.18	"	"	"	"	"	"	"
Lv } Omaha	8.35	"	"	"	"	"	"	"
Ar Chicago	9.25	Wed	Thu	Fri	Sat	Sun	Mon	Tue
Lv Seattle	9.40	Sat	Sun	Mon	Tue	Wed	Thu	Fri
" Tacoma	11.45							
" Portland	9.15	Sun	Mon	Tue	Wed	Thu	Fri	Sat
" Spokane	7.25	"	"	"	"	"	"	"
" Baker City	11.15	"	"	"	"	"	"	"
Ar Green River	9.10	Mon	Tue	Wed	Thu	Fri	Sat	Sun
Ar Chicago	9.25	Wed	Thu	Fri	Sat	Sun	Mon	Tue
	A M							

The Overland Limited, Electric Lighted Throughout—Standard sleeper San Francisco to Chicago, connecting at Sacramento with buffet sleeper from Los Angeles. Observation car and buffet-library car, with barber shop and bath. San Francisco to Omaha. Composite-observation car and coaches Omaha to Chicago. Through passengers from Portland and North Pacific Coast points transfer to Chicago sleeper at Green River. All meals in dining cars.

But whether it left Chicago over the rails of the Milwaukee, as is demonstrated on these and the preceding pages, or on the left hand track of the Chicago & North Western, the main section of *The Overland Limited* was a distinguishing hallmark of the Union Pacific everywhere west of Omaha. When, in the winter of 1907, it was photographed as shown here by the invaluable Fred Jukes just out of Rawlins, Wyoming, it carried the conventional head-end mail storage car, a combination baggage and smoking car with its barber shop and other amenities of de luxe travel, four regularly assigned Pullman sleepers of varying floor plan, a diner and the observation-lounge with brass railed platform at the end.

During the brief interlude when *The Overland* was the special pride of the Milwaukee it left Chicago from the old Union Depot shown at the right in an age when the vast wardrobe trunks of voyagers shared the driver's box of a two horse growler parked at the curb. Specially assigned Pullman sleepers such as *Glenview* and *Dakota* were built by Pullman to the Milwaukee's order and carried both the carrier's initials and the magic name of *The Overland Limited* on their name boards as testimony to the brief but splendid love affair between the train and the road that for a short time enjoyed its affections. *(Right: Milwaukee Railroad; Below, Two Photos: Arthur D. Dubin Collection.)*

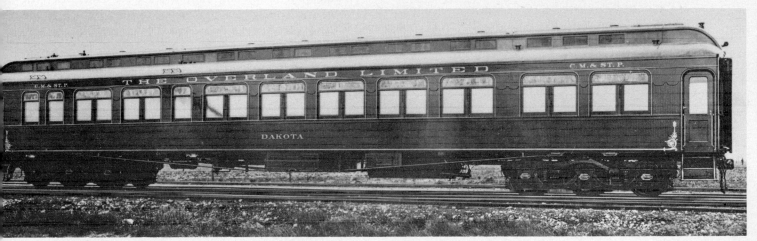

Westbound it was about the same as 1900—arrival in Ogden at 2:35 P.M. and out at 4:50 P.M. for San Francisco.

Gerald Best rode the Rio Grande-Rock Island sleeper in 1927 and reported that the pause in Denver was just enough to accommodate passengers who wished to go uptown for dinner and a round or two of cocktails at the Navarre, the town's most elite speakeasy of the time, before dining in grandeur at the Brown Palace Hotel just across the street.

Legend and folklore cluster thickly about *The Overland's* name in the West, lacking perhaps the perfumed overtones of *The Chief* and *Super-Chief* with their roster of glamour names, but extending in greater depth of time into the storied past and regional mythology.

Gertrude Atherton recalled that when the Duke of Manchester visited San Francisco accompanied by his son the Viscount Mandeville, the younger Englishman was so strongly impressed with having read Bret Harte and other frontier writers of California fiction that he persistently believed in the pioneer character of the country he was visiting long after the last Sioux war party had been taken to a reservation. The Viscount, in defiance of the conventions which required a nice attention to clothes on the part of gentlemen, insisted on appearing aboard the cars in mining camp attire, red flannel shirt, thigh boots and a six-shooter in his belt, much to the amusement of more sophisticated voyagers.

Gertrude Atherton herself, a haughty aristocrat by virtue of one generation's precedence in San Francisco society, hardly ever emerged from her stateroom between Oakland Mole and Chicago, and if she did at all, it was heavily veiled and accompanied by a tiring maid when she took a constitutional stroll on the depot platform at Laramie or Green River.

Nellie Melba, at the height of her operatic fame as the most aloof and highly recompensed singer in the world, begged the *Overland* dining car steward, as an act of mercy, not to serve Peach Melba when dinner was sent to her drawing room. Her fame as a diva and that of the dessert created in her name by the great Escoffier were about equal and no chef, anywhere and given the opportunity, could resist trying his hand at it. Dame Nellie complained that she had Peach Melba running out of her ears.

Most of the pronounced characteristics of *Overland* patrons and their mild eccentricities were of a benevolent order to evoke more amusement than consternation among train crews. Such was not the case with Mrs. Francis J. Carolan, daughter-in-law of George Mortimer Pullman, and one of the most arrogant and demanding San Francisco hostesses of the decades immediately after the turn of the century.

Mrs. Carolan, suffering from an imagined social affront on the part of members of the Crocker family who, in turn, were of course heirs to vast sums of Southern Pacific money, erected at Hillsborough during the opening years of the first world war an immense marble chateau whose cost, magnificence and many imposing splendors were calculated to put the conservative Crockers completely in their place, which was in the social shade of Peninsula high life. Following the seizure of the railroads by the Federal government in 1917, Pullman stock suffered heavy reverses. Mrs. Carolan was unable to maintain the vast establishment in the style she demanded and spent more and more of her time in New York to which, in an age before the flying machine, she was forced to commute aboard *The Overland Limited*.

Taking *The Overland* constituted a double affront to the testy heiress. It represented the railroad which had so richly endowed her rivals for social supremacy and also the detestable Pullman Company which, although it had made her incredibly rich, had failed her in her hour of greatest need of dividends.

"I was a stenographer on *The Overland Limited*," a woman now living in retirement at San Leandro recently told Millie Robbins of *The San Francisco Chronicle*, "and several times had the bad luck to encounter Mrs. Carolan, who went to Chicago frequently, on the train. To my mind she had the world's worst temper.

"The first thing she did on entering her drawing room was to tear all the sheets and pillow cases, blankets and towels from their place and throw them into the aisle. Then she would send for me and instruct me to take a telegram to the trainmaster at Sacramento ordering him to buy some plain linen and have it placed on board when we stopped there.

"'I refuse to sleep between sheets advertising the Pullman Company,' she stormed.

"Nothing happened at Sacramento and she loudly declared she was going to have me fired. On arriving at Chicago I made my report, but was told by my employers in the Pullman Company to forget it, as she invariably had the entire train crew discharged on every trip she made for one reason or another. Nothing ever happened.

"When her husband went East, he'd always take *The Pacific Limited* which in those days followed *The Overland,* to avoid having to put up with her scenes and tantrums. He was a very nice old gentleman and raised orchids as a hobby."

Scott Newhall, member of a long established family of California pioneers for whom the community of Newhall is named, recalled that as a schoolboy going East in the thirties and making round trips at Christmas and Easter, the highlight of his vacations was the adventure of riding *The Overland.*

"All the boys of my age who regularly went East to school knew the train crews by name and dining car stewards were often specially instructed to look out for them, a duty they faithfully fulfilled to their endearment to our parents," he says in reminiscence. "We knew the names of the regularly assigned sleepers and I remember them now: *Oakland, Centridge, Alazon, Poplar Dale, Overland* and *Overview*. There was also an observation car that was a great favorite with all of us because the colored boy in charge was specially expert at removing cinders from our eyes after we'd been riding the platform. If memory serves, there were vestigial traces of air conditioning in those days, but we invariably arrived sooty and covered with pieces of roadbed picked up looking out the car half-doors at Cheyenne and Echo Canyon."

Some three decades before Mr. Newhall was an *Overland* regular, its train crew had been set by the ears by the presence on the sailing list of Prince Andre Poniatowski, son of the Master of Horse to Napoleon III and a direct descendant of King Stanislaus of Poland who was coming West to make an auspicious marriage among the well placed California heiresses then available in such abundance. Prince Poniatowski, with commendable sentiments

of democracy, refused to have meals sent back to his private room and cheerfully dined and lunched with less exalted patrons in the dining car. Each morning, however, he commanded a quart of White Seal champagne to be served while he was shaving, a minute quantity of which was utilized for brushing his teeth and the rest of which was consumed as princely refreshment. It reinforced his determination to republican conduct generally.

Although several generations of *Overland* passengers seem to have avoided cutting their throats in an age innocent of safety razors, there were patrons who felt that wielding a straight Solingen blade against their windpipe at seventy miles an hour presented a hazard it might be prudent to avoid and arrived at either terminal with three days beard to show for it. One such within the memory of the author was Massachusetts' well-remembered Senator David Ignatius Walsh who still favored a straight razor but was unwilling to risk its use in transit or even to patronize the comparatively expert ministration of the train barber.

"God has watched over me for seventy years with what I construe to be benevolence," the solon deposed in the train bar while rubbing an appraising hand over the stubble. "But there's such a thing as tempting Providence too far and I'm not taking that chance."

In *The Overland's* early days, just as its departure eastbound was an event in which San Francisco participated as a pleasant and recurrent ritual, so its arrival from the East was made memorable for passengers. When *The Overland's* connecting ferry docked at the foot of Market Street its travel-weary occupants, instead of being subjected to the vociferous harrassments of cab drivers and hotel runners as was the universal custom elsewhere in America at the time, were met by representatives of the town's leading hotels of a notable deferential order. Beautifully mannered Chinese in ceremonial robes greeted them with baskets of fresh California fruits and flowers and the best vintages of California wines suitably chilled for dusty palates. Their patronage was solicited in subdued and deferential tones and promises of the best of everything extended in courtly terms. The Palace, Lucky Baldwin's, The Metropolitan and The Occidental made a good impression from the first. San Francisco did things in style.

Sometime in the thirties, Ethel Barrymore, who invariably traveled in the grand manner of an earlier generation and occupied two drawing rooms banked with flowers and furnished with her own sofa pillows and framed portraits of royal personages all arranged by her personal maid, got a nasty turn on re-entering her suite after an excursion to the diner. In passing through Chicago she had put up at the Ambassador Hotel whose proprietor, the celebrated Ernie Byfield, had presented her, along with more substantial refreshments for the voyage, with a couple of samples of his latest proprietary product called College Inn Tomato Juice Cocktails. Tomato juice was just emerging on the national awareness as a morning after restorative and the Byfield version, being in its early stages of manufacture, had been imperfectly processed. In Miss Barrymore's absence the containers had exploded spattering the drawing room with a reasonable facsimile of human gore. Her shrieks of dismay brought the train crew running and it took considerable persuasion to reassure her that a sensational murder hadn't been committed in her absence.

The drama and tragedy of the San Francisco fire and earthquake of April 18, 1906, always afterward established in the popular imagination as a turning point in history so that "before The Fire" became San Francisco's Golden Age in recollection, also rode *The Overland*.

The New York Metropolitan Opera Company was at the time paying its annual visit to San Francisco and the evening previous, in what was later to be recognized as the swan song of an era, Caruso had sung the part of Don Jose in "Carmen" to the most glittering audience in the memory of local society reporters. Most of the opera company were staying at The Palace and when, at five in the morning of Wednesday, April 18th, the San Andreas Fault shook the city on its foundations "as a terrier shakes a rat," singers, directors and other members of the troupe were driven to the street, many still in evening dress, having just returned from parties in their honor throughout the Nob Hill region.

Legend has it that Caruso, clad only in one of the hotel's bath towels and clutching under his arm a signed portrait of Theodore Roosevelt tore through the shaken guests in the lobby screaming "Give me Vesuvius!" Later in the day the members of the company foregathered in the safety afforded by one of the city's open squares hoping the flames might be abated so that they could go on with their repertory. One of the first casualties of the quake, however, had been the opera house and by the 19th the Metropolitan troupers were seeking a way to get out of town with whatever they had salvaged in the initial panic.

Oakland, of course, was intact and the Southern Pacific, although its operations elsewhere the length of California were in a state of chaos, was still running its Overland trains. Word was passed to the stars and their dependents that a sleeping car had been added to the *Overland* and that they were to assemble at The Mole at train time that afternoon. Adolphus Busch, the St. Louis beer magnate, had arranged to have his splendid private car *Adolphus* coupled to the train but the Met singers could get no private car and were glad of any accommodations at all. Ernest Goerlitz, a member of the troupe, contrived to hire a steam launch to get his fellows across the Bay where ferries had long since ceased to run, and when they counted noses on the platform everybody was present but Caruso. At the last moment he showed up still with the portrait of Roosevelt but in more suitable traveling attire than that in which he had fled his Palace suite. He had used the photograph as a sort of passport to get him through the fire lines and the military now ringing the city.

Few of the company were dressed for transcontinental travel. Madame Josephine Jacoby was wearing her nightgown and a pair of gold slippers that were part of her costume of the night before. Pol Henri Plancon was formally dressed in a silk top hat and morning clothes with a boutonniere in his buttonhole, but he had been unable to dye his beard, which was now a bright green. Louise Homer was wearing the trousers to her husband's evening clothes and a diamond dog collar, Emma Eames was fully costumed for "Aida" and Alfred Hertz, the company manager, was visibly pleased with himself and carried four bottles of the best brandy under his arm. He had spent the day before in the Palace bar until the building was almost consumed and had salvaged all he could carry on leaving.

The departure of *The Overland* was delayed a few moments while the baritone Campanari gave a brief interview to the Associated Press consisting of the sentiment: "It is all such a change." Walter Lord, a historian of the fire, felt it was a triumph of understatement.

As the train passed along the Oakland waterfront, the departing artists had a fine view of the flaming city from their compartment windows.

Almost as spectacular and nowhere nearly as disastrous was the view afforded *Overland* passengers two years later when The Great White Fleet sailed through the Golden Gate on its way to the orient and anchored in splendor within easy view of all Southern Pacific trains arriving at Oakland Mole. San Francisco, a chaos of excitement as it recovered from the fire and earthquake, went mad with patriotic delight as the sixteen battleships came up the harbor. The town spread itself; there was a $20 a plate dinner for the officers, a fabulous sum for the time, and a ball remembered by old timers even to this day which went on at the newly reopened Fairmont Hotel on Nob Hill without interruption for 48 hours. To participate in these gala doings the Southern Pacific ran no fewer than sixty special trains to San Francisco some originating as far away as Portland, and an enterprising staff photographer took a fine view of *The Overland* steaming out of Sixteenth Street yards with the battleship *Iowa* in the background which was ultimately made into a picture postcard and sold over a million copies.

Over the years *The Overland* became timeless, venerable, institutional, one in the awareness of Californians with memories of the Bear Flag, gold coinage, Comstock millionaires and the earthquake and fire of 1906. San Franciscans who had made their wedding trips aboard its cars saw their children as newly married couples wave farewell from its observation platform. Its sailings from Oakland Mole until comparatively recently were events, not as stately perhaps as the red carpet departures of *The 20th Century Limited* from Grand Central, but implicit with even greater distances and farther landfarings.

In the middle thirties No. 27 was scheduled to pause at Reno at ten in the evening and, because much of the car servicing was then done there instead of at Sparks and the train was on a more leisurely schedule anyway, it often remained blocking traffic on North Center Street for half an hour

or more. This was sufficient time for many adventurous passengers to get down from the Pullmans and step into the Bank Club which was just across the street for a whirl at roulette or the dice tables while the mail was loaded. As departure loomed, the engineer wound a mighty blast on his whistle and the Bank bartenders and dealers set up a clamorous outcry of "*Overland* leaving," much as theater doormen shout "Curtain going up," while the patrons raced for the train leaking silver dollars as they ran.

Eastbound No. 28 in those days left Oakland at 8:30 in the evening and it was the pleasant custom of many people to have dinner with departing friends in their stateroom or the diner and get off at Martinez to take a convenient local back to town. During prohibition when patriotism placed a premium on powerful bottle doings, tarriers sometimes got carried off to Sacramento or even Reno.

Right up to the time of the 1941 war *The Overland* was widely known as a fun train.

Always an institutional landmark in the West, *The Overland* was regarded as a household name in California and a legend of reliability amongst members of the Southern Pacific family of loyal retainers. Other crack trains in the land such as the New Haven's *Merchants' Limited*, the New York Central's *Twentieth Century Limited*, *The Queen & Crescent* on the Louisville & Nashville and the Lehigh Valley's *Black Diamond* occupied positions of esteem in the countryside they served. Along the route of the Chesapeake & Ohio, farmers quite literally for years set their clocks by the passing of the *George Washington* and year after year conservative summer residents of the nation's most conservative seasonal resort rode Down East aboard the Maine Central's *Bar Harbor Express*. *The Overland* was in this category, one of the good familiar things by which folk set their clocks and whose whistle on the Great Plains was reassurance that all was for the best in a well ordered universe.

Gordon Pates, managing editor of *The San Francisco Chronicle*, also a familiar property on Nob Hill and the perfumed purlieus of Hillsborough, Atherton and Tiburon, recalls the dominant position the train occupied in the ancestral scheme of things in his family.

"My uncle, E. E. Ryder, now living in honorable retirement at Alameda," writes Pates, "worked nearly fifty years for the Southern Pacific. He began as an office boy in the days before child labor laws blighted our economy and ended as administrative head of the dining car department.

"I dined at his table often as a child and was raised on tales of the mighty Espee. Most of these, in retrospect, seem to have dealt with that vast body of dining car employees my uncle was pleased to identify in those more relaxed days as coons. I early formed the opinion that they were a temperamental lot as gifted at carving each other up as turning out the cuisine for which S. P. diners were famous.

"In my vision of life aboard the diner, the crisp linen and polished silver was always accompanied by the copious flow of blood in the galley as the train roared through the night toward Ogden. I recall one Sunday dinner conversation which detailed in bloody fashion a fierce fracas aboard *The Overland* in which two gentlemen of color had a falling out over the results of a dice game. At an emergency stop somewhere between Sparks and Ogden, a tolerant undertaker bore off the loser and sheriff's deputies put the arm on the winner. One night also, as I recall, the diner on the *Cascade Limited* northbound for Portland was enlivened by a galley battle which resulted in one of the participants being hurled into the night as the train passed over the Siskiyous. I do not now recollect if he was ever recovered.

"These differences of opinion reduced to laconic telegrams eventually found their way into the "in" box on my uncle's desk at 65 Market Street and from there home to provide an answer to the common question, 'What happened at the office today?'

"Whenever I had occasion to ride *The Overland* myself, dining car stewards and waiters invariably showered me with the kindnesses reserved for relatives of the line's executives. These I acknowledged somewhat gingerly, since I was never sure when kindness might turn into aggravated assault. Needless to say, it never did but I was completely convinced that each of the waiters and cooks carried under his spotless white coat a cleaver with which to settle such arguments as might arise. I must say it made dining an adventure and at the end of each trip brought a sense of satisfaction that one had escaped with his life.

"Around our house we used to say S. P. the way people now say U. S. and it meant almost the same thing as we owed our three squares a day to the largess of this powerful institution."

Alfred Knopf, the famous New York publisher and intimate of the literary great of the world, recalls settling down in an over-stuffed armchair in an *Overland* lounge after a bounteous dinner the first night out of Chicago. He courteously offered his cigar case to the well dressed gentleman in the adjacent seat, explaining so that the recipient might be under no misapprehension of its quality, that the cigar was an Upmann Special.

"Nobody but Upmann gets Upmann Specials," said the gentlemen gruffly. "I'm Upmann."

Note has been made previously of the courtly reception accorded Southern Pacific passengers by the hotel managements of the San Francisco nineties when they arrived at Oakland Mole to board the ferry. At the other end of the run when *The Overland* docked at the Chicago & North Western's old Wells Street station a somewhat similar ceremony awaited the passengers who got down from its Pullmans. All trains were met by two classes of carriage for their transport to hotels or other railway terminals, the town's professional free-lance horsecab drivers and the immemorial omnibuses of Parmalee Transfer. *The Overland* was met by a third delegation in the form of a rank of gleaming and immaculately maintained hansom carriages in the employ of Marshall Field, ready to drive them directly to Chicago's most celebrated landmark and shopping Mecca. Well-to-do visitors from the West often wanted to go right off to Marshall Field and the best heeled of them arrived, of course, on *The Overland*.

The night crossing of Nevada on *The Overland* was a trip conducive to tranquil repose and untroubled sleep. The Southern Pacific operation, never at a very accelerated pace over a magnificent roadbed and long tangents and vast sweeping curves, was soporific in the extreme. The seasoned traveler knew where he was instinctively: first the restricted speed and hollow rumble of the Lucin trestle, then the relatively fast tangents across the salt flats to Montello and again the slower ascent of the east grade of the Ruby Mountains. Nor was the experienced *Overland* passenger ever at a loss to identify his whereabouts if the raising of his stateroom shade failed to disclose a depot and it usually didn't, since the Pullmans halted far out in the yards. Nevada, seldom troubled with superficial aspects of morality, tolerated red light districts as a matter of local option and mostly the option was exercised. If, hard by the tracks, a blaze of Neon trim and six foot letters announced that the Coq Rouge was in business, the enlightened occupant of Bedroom D knew he was in Elko. If the night sky was dominated by the advertised presence of the Why Not, he was in Winnemucca, always a town famed for its relaxed attitudes and absence of prudery. If the business shingle announced simply Ida's Place, he was in Wells.

Carlin alone failed in the matter of facile identification. It was an operational stop only where the cars were watered and brake rigging inspected and, as far as the author was ever able to determine, had no distinguishing bagnio to tell the briefly wakened voyager where he was.

During the 1941 war when the theater of operations was shifting to the Pacific and the entire world of military personnel, politics, logistics and allied civilian activity was turning its face westward, *The Overland* ran in two sections as a regular thing with twenty cars to a train. The preferred way to get from Chicago to San Francisco was on the *City* and the section of the *City* in greatest request was that whose diner boasted the presence of Wild Bill Kurthy as steward. Kurthy, as tempestuous a personality as ever graced the Old West, somehow saw to it that, although rationing might be in effect elsewhere, it was never even heard of on the dining cars under his chaotic jurisdiction. Filets dripped with melted butter, thick cream was available in Niagaras, everything you couldn't get elsewhere appeared in limitless quantities on Kurthy's diner and was urged on the delighted or terrified passengers with a threatening hospitality that brooked no denial. On retiring, favored passengers were apt to find that the buzzer on the door heralded the arrival of a beaming darky with a mound of rare cold roast beef sandwiches lest the traveler, already dined to satiety on Porterhouse and rich pastry, should feel faint in the night.

"The Wild Man will kill me if you don't eat them," the bearer would announce.

No such sumptuous plenty was available on *The Overland,* but train crews had a way of looking out

for old customers and the suggestion that perhaps you'd like dinner served in your room was a hint that forbidden double lamb chops or New York cuts would be found nesting under the nappery.

The author had occasion to cross the continent repeatedly during the years of hostility when rationing was taken seriously in California even if it wasn't anywhere else, and made it a practice to pick up five or ten pounds of the best creamery butter while passing through Chicago with which to make friends and influence people along the way. The word, discreetly circulated by the dining car steward, that he was custodian of such treasure in his cold box worked wonders in the way of improved sleeping accommodations if the train was full, which it usually was.

On one westward trip, aboard *The Overland* on which the author had been, despite influence in the highest places, unable to get sleeping space, he boarded the train with a first class ticket and was undertaking to bargain with the Pullman conductor for a full length divan in the club car for the night. A gentleman across the aisle, hitherto concealed behind a copy of *The Chicago News*, put down his paper to reveal the presence of Eugene Meyer, wealthy and influential owner of the *Washington Post*. Recognizing a fellow newspaperman, albeit in a somewhat less elevated echelon, in distress, Mr. Meyer courteously allowed that he had two adjoining staterooms and that one of them was available if the beneficiary of this windfall would share it with its present occupant.

Investigation revealed that Mr. Meyer was accompanied by a carcass of the best Chicago beef suspended from the upper berth and traveling as a wartime gift to Henry Kaiser. The reporter was delighted to share the compartment with the assorted minute steaks, rib ends and filets all the way to Oakland Mole.

Jake Ehrlich, long and widely known as one of the most sensationally successful trial lawyers of the West Coast was, in *The Overland's* lifetime a devoted partisan of the train both on professional and personal grounds.

"First and foremost, it was the only thinkable way for anyone of importance to travel when going East. As a hallmark of prestige in California it was easily of the same rank as *The Century* out of New York," he says, "but I had only the warmest personal recollections of its crew and overall conduct as well.

"Back in 1925 I had been practicing law only three years when my wife's folks in the East sent her carfare to come on for a visit. They wanted to see the children and couldn't come out themselves, so I ponied up $50 for her incidental expenses, a lot of money for me then, and went over to Oakland to see her off. I had two silver dollars in my pocket in addition, and these I gave to the porter on their sleeping car with instruction for their special care and any little favors that were within his gift.

"A week or ten days later he called at my San Francisco office and gave me an hour by hour account of their trip, what they had done and said all along the route, and I swear everything but what they had ordered in the diner. I couldn't have obtained such a reliable report from the most expensive private detective. He refused another tip. Just said it was part of his job and he liked to do nice things for friends of the Southern Pacific. They don't come like that nowadays, I guess."

A less favorable recollection of experience with *The Overland* was the time an imposter masquerading under Ehrlich's name at the time of his greatest fame as a barrister insinuated himself into the confidence of a married woman on *The Overland* to such good effect that she gave him all the money she had about her and, when they arrived in Chicago, the family car. Her outraged husband called on Ehrlich for restitution and together they traced the miscreant and had him jailed.

"I was naturally vexed at being impersonated by a scoundrel," says Ehrlich, "but what made me really cross was that the fellow was a low sneaky type, not nearly as good looking as I then was. I told the woman in future not to believe anybody who said he was Jake Ehrlich unless he looked like John Barrymore."

As it was to many other San Franciscans in the golden years of its going, *The Overland* is remembered "as a part of my very existence" by Dorothy Liebes, the highly talented member of an already talented California family who is one of the most stylish (and expensive) of all decorative designers in New York.

"I went East to school on it every fall for years and years," Mrs. Liebes recalls, "and then came home through Canada on the Canadian Pacific all on the same round-trip ticket. People always saw us off in those days with masses of bon voyage presents, most of which were eminently unsuited to railroad travel, like orchids and gardenias, so I got the bright idea of dashing off the train when it stopped at Sacramento to give my flowers to the Western Union telegraph girls. This was the beginning of a beautiful friendship which ended, like so many precedents, in being a mild sort of obligation because I felt I *had* to get down every time I passed through, hand her the flowers and hope she was going to a party that night."

Mrs. Liebes' most hilarious recollection of *The Overland* was on the occasion of the first appearance of shower baths as part of the train's luxury equipment, a date she prudently refrains from recalling.

"Until that time," she writes, "in hot weather we had to keep the windows of our staterooms open, even though it entailed covering our faces with towels wrung out in cold water or witch hazel in order to endure the blast of hot air crossing the prairies. The shower was immediately in great demand but I, being the clever, conniving type, managed to be first in line when it was opened for service. Much to my joy, there was a huge pile of snowy clean bathtowels stacked on the little bench in the dressing room. So I put one on the floor for a bath mat, dried one leg with another, the other leg with a third and altogether used up five lovely towels.

"When I came to pay the attendant, however, he informed me that shower charges were based on the towel consumption involved — like the saucers at a sidewalk cafe in Paris — and that my bill, based on a charge of six bits per towel, was $3.75. The shock was a not inconsiderable one, considering the availability of money in those days and my schoolgirl status, but I always say, live and learn."

Merle Armitage, for many years an impresario closely associated with the great of the world of opera and concerts who traveled widely on a continental dimension in the interest of such clients as Mary Garden, Paderewski and Anna Pavlova, often rode *The Overland* in its glory days and is a fund of anecdotal reminiscences of life on the cars with Rosa Ponselle, John Charles Thomas and Mischa Elman.

"In 1920 my partner and I booked the great tenor, John McCormack for an extensive tour in Australia and New Zealand," he writes, "and when he had terminated his contract, the ship on which he was to return was due in San Francisco on December 19th, which would allow McCormack, his accompanist Edwin Schneider, and our representative with him, Howard Potter, to reach New York in time for Christmas, where Mrs. McCormack was preparing a special celebration.

"I went to San Francisco from New York to greet the party and escort them back to New York. But there was a heavy storm in the Pacific, and the ship was delayed several days.

"When it became apparent that Christmas in New York was impossible, I counselled with my friend Paul Shoup, of the Southern Pacific. Shoup was very sympathetic, and together we planned the following strategy. We telephoned Mrs. McCormack in New York, told her that it would be impossible for John to be home for Christmas, and suggested that she bring the two children, and the presents, and meet us halfway across the continent.

"Just as soon as we had a definite docking time for the ship, we made the following arrangements. Mrs. McCormack took a train that would land her in Ogden, Utah the day before Christmas. We in the meantime booked a drawing room for McCormack on the appropriate departure day of the *Overland Limited,* and without him knowing it, we also reserved the drawing room next door.

"In the extra drawing room, we installed a Christmas tree, suitably decorated and with electric candles. I purchased a number of presents and we hung holly wreaths around, and made the room very festive indeed.

"In Ogden on Christmas day, we took John to the back of the train, on the pretext of showing him something from the rear observation platform, a standard feature of *The Overland.* This allowed Mrs. McCormack, the two children and the dozen or more presents she had brought, to be stealthily moved into the drawing room next door to John's. This included a case of Mumms extra dry.

"At a proper moment, a porter opened the door between the rooms. John had been reading, but the opening of the door interested him, and when he looked into the room and saw his wife and children, he was certain it was an apparition, or a

miracle. He covered his eyes with his hands, and shouted, 'My God, it's not true!'

"But of course it was true, and John often said it was the happiest surprise of his life, and the best Christmas. The *Overland Limited* crew entered sympathetically and enthusiastically into the scheme. That night, the chef and the dining car steward, served a little pig, roasted golden brown, with an apple in his mouth, and the sumptuous meal closed with the largest plum pudding I have ever seen, flambé.

"The whole affair was so successful, that Mr. Shoup ordered a Christmas tree to be placed in the club observation car, on every Christmas day thereafter, for the lonely souls caught away from home on Christmas."

Less amiable in its overtones was the time Mr. Armitage, in the role of impresario-courier to Yvette Guilbert, a temperamental French music hall *diseuse* with a reputation for being a fantastic concert attraction and poison to managers and all associated with her, took on a tour of the West.

Mr. Armitage undertook to chaperone her across country to San Francisco aboard *The Overland* and life was a burden to him from the moment they highballed out of Chicago. The food was too rich, the servants didn't speak French, the wine card didn't have her favorite vintage of Bordeaux and, worst of all, as they sped westward there were a lot of rich looking cities which had not been included by Mr. Armitage in her concert schedule. Why had she not been booked in Davenport, in Omaha, in North Platte, in Cheyenne? In vain the manager explained that a sophisticated Continental who spoke no English would get scant reception in cow towns of the West and what she received would not be favorable.

"Everybody in the world knows Yvette Guilbert," she told him crossly, "and all people of culture and refinement understand French. Even in America."

Things became really rough after *The Overland* left Cheyenne. It was midwinter, snow was falling heavily and there was a motive power shortage. Whatever was assigned the train for the grade over Sherman was insufficient and shortly it was stalled in a vast drift in a windy cut with snow banking up to the window ledges.

The Guilbert sent for Mr. Armitage again. Did he know what he had done? He had taken the finest artist in the entire concert world into this damnable American wilderness where they would soon find their graves. They were doomed. Starvation would shortly set in and then the Indians would attack. She knew all about it. She had been reading American literature and knew how savage conditions were on the Great Plains.

"At this juncture, as God is my judge," deposes Mr. Armitage, "she produced the book that assured her her scalp was as good as lifted. It was 'The Last of the Mohicans.'"

Mr. Armitage barricaded himself in his stateroom with a bottle of Bourbon, a prey to gloomy thoughts until a rotary was brought up from Laramie and they were on their way again, if not exactly rejoicing. Next day an emotional thaw as well set in. Mlle. Guilbert discovered that, among its other facilities, *The Overland* had a ladies' bath.

"Just imagine, a real hot tub bath at seventy miles an hour in the middle of nowhere! You Americans really are darlings!"

Her run in San Francisco was a smash, so much so that when their time ran out at the Curran Theater they moved for two more weeks into the happily vacant Geary. Mlle. Guilbert stayed at the St. Francis. Mr. Armitage put up at The Palace. He felt it was far enough away for a reasonable degree of safety.

On still another occasion, Mr. Armitage was chaperone on *The Overland* to something not French and not temperamental, and a great deal more satisfactory from any angle. In 1914 he was in the employ of the Packard Motor Car Company in Detroit as art and technical adviser in the typography and layouts of its house organ *The Packard Magazine*.

"It really was a sort of super house organ and I was retained to go to Detroit twice a month to package a truly smart news and picture magazine to extoll the Packard product," he remembers. "A Packard 6-48 Phaeton, a long, low, chic model, had just won the Concours d'Elegance in Paris, and now the company wanted to demonstrate its ruggedness and strength. Win the women with style and the men with endurance!

"A site in the remote Grand Teton mountains of Wyoming was selected and a camp established.

Here, the car would be put through its paces. Because the middle west had nothing but muddy dirt wagon roads, it was decided to ship the Packard Phaeton to the point on the Union Pacific railroad nearest the Teton country, which was Rock Springs, Wyoming.

"As editor and designer of the new magazine, this project fired my imagination. At the time the famous *Overland Limited* was very much in the news. Why not ship the Phaeton west on that celebrated train? The company accepted the idea, and then I began to elaborate on it. Why not ship it, ready to run, in a baggage car of its own, and why not have that baggage car an example of all the amenities of camping in the glorious West? Well, why not, said President Henry B. Joy, a wealthy Detroiter who had bought into the Packard company in its second year. Joy gave me the green light, and we had an *Overland Limited* baggage car brought to Detroit, and parked as near as possible to the Packard factory.

"First, we had canvas tacked all over the interior of the car, and pulled tight to make a base for mural painting. Then a member of the Detroit Institute of Arts staff, painted rocky mountains, rivers, lakes and forests completely around the interior. The Packard Phaeton, complete with hampers, luggage, and every conceivable accessory, was installed at the far end of the car, and made fast. To see the car, one had to traverse an area of tents, all erected and ready for sleeping, pseudo campfires, guns, fishing tackle, etc. A camper's paradise. And there at the far end was the blue, elegant car, with its yellow artillery wheels, Italian leather upholstery, and shining brass.

We arranged with the railways involved, the North Western, the Union Pacific, and the Southern Pacific, to place this baggage between the club-buffet car, which was standard equipment, and the diner. A souvenir booklet was prepared, presenting the Packard Phaeton, courtesy the *Overland Limited,* and each passenger was handed one as he passed through.

"Needless to say, it was a sensation, with a surprise ending.

"Before we arrived at Rock Springs, where the baggage car was to be cut off, we received a telegram from the President of the Union Pacific, ordering the car with its exhibit to continue on to

San Francisco, where the Earl C. Anthony organization would exhibit it for three days. So on to San Francisco it went, on the *Overland,* not to return for its endurance trials for a full week."

Beginning in mid-February of 1915 *The Overland's* component carriers made a very nice thing indeed out of the Panama-Pacific International Exposition held at San Francisco and celebrating the dedication of the Panama canal, an event which boded no good at all for their freight departments which were interested in the transport of heavy merchandise between ports now available to shortened sea lanes.

The train was all-Pullman, extra-fare at the time and brought to the Oakland Mole a wide variety of name passengers ranging from Fritz Kreisler and the dancer Loie Fuller to Mrs. William Howard Taft, Lady Aberdeen, Mrs. John Hays Hammond and Mrs. William Gibbs McAdoo, whose husband, President Wilson's inept appointee was shortly to make a shambles of every carrier in the land as their wartime administrator.

Fred Juke's photographs of the period showing *The Overland* running as Trains Nos. 1 and 2 on the Southern Pacific depict it with a classic consist of one or two head-end revenue cars, a mail storage and R. P. O., followed by a combination baggage-buffet, three, four or five Pullman Standard sleepers, a Southern Pacific diner, and brass railed observation lounge which might owe its origins to any of the three carrying railroads, Espee, U. P., or North Western.

Although traffic for San Francisco's 1939 fair, the Golden Gate International Exposition at Treasure Island was far heavier than it had been in 1915, *The Overland* was less a beneficiary of it because the flow of passengers was in large measure diverted to two strictly de luxe competing trains over the same routing, *The Forty-Niner* and *Treasure Island Special.* By this time, too, the streamlined, Diesel-powered *City of San Francisco* was running on a five trips a month basis between Chicago and California, while the overflow from this multiplicity of services rode in less style but still solid comfort aboard *The Pacific Limited.*

For a brief period covering the two and a half years between April 1935 and September 1937, an element of chaos, already a notable component in the operations record of *The Overland* was intro-

duced into the train's history by the presence on the Southern Pacific's timecard of an *Advance Overland Limited* supplementing Trains Nos. 27 and 28 between Oakland and Ogden and then merging with the main section east of Ogden on the Union Pacific and the North Western.

Southern Pacific Train No. 30, *The Advance San Francisco Overland,* to give its full title, commenced operations out of Oakland Mole in April 1935 with a full complement of conventional *Overland* equipment head-end revenue, tourist and Standard Pullman sleepers, chair cars, diner and a panache of elegance in the form of a brass railed observation car which automatically gave it the status of a ranking name train. *The Advance San Francisco Overland* was not merely an extra section of a regularly scheduled varnish but a separate and identifiable operation in its own right just as *The Advance Twentieth Century Limited* was on the New York Central until the coming of *The Commodore Vanderbilt.*

The westbound *Advance San Francisco Overland* wasn't inaugurated until December 13, 1936 running as Train No. 9-287. Both train numbers were changed in the ensuing months, but the varnish haul retained its identity until September 15, 1937 when *The Challenger* made its first run and *The Advance Overland* became a memory.

Because *The Advance San Francisco Overland* ceased to run beyond Ogden its existence has been doubted by students of railroading, a scepticism that was naturally encouraged by the absence of any mention of it in the operating schedules of connecting carriers. It nevertheless once ran with its own smokebox numbers and drumhead insigne at the rear, as is attested by photographs at an appropriate place in this volume. It is a minor footnote of irony that the carrier which was the last to recognize the magic of *The Overland* name was the only one of the three railroads over which it ran during its long and useful life to see potentialities of merit in an extension of that name to another train. Over the Union Pacific and the North Western where *The Overland* had first emerged, it ran merely as extra sections of a train already established on the operating timecard.

In its glory years as an extra fare and truly limited train, *The Overland* established a firm rule against the carriage of special equipment, meaning

Excepting only *The Twentieth Century Limited*, which Walter Gieseking described as "my gentleman's club when I am in the United States," no train in the record knew the presence of more celebrities than *The Overland* in its splendid years. Until the emergence of the films in the nineteen twenties, few names that made news had occasion to visit Los Angeles, and San Francisco was the social, financial and professional capital of the Pacific Coast. Arriving at Oakland aboard *The Overland* on their way to The Palace Hotel were the Grand Duke Boris, William Jennings Bryan, Lady Randolph Churchill, Mrs. Harry Payne Whitney, Prince Albert of the Belgians and Presidents McKinley, Roosevelt and William Howard Taft. It carried the private cars of *(left to right above)* President McKinley shown greeting admirers at Oakland, John Pierpont Morgan, when he wasn't traveling in an entire chartered train of Anglican bishops, the glamorous Lily Langtry (Lady de Bathe aboard her private car *Lalee* which a contemporary described as being "voluptuous as Cleopatra's barge without sails"), and William K. Vanderbilt who married the daughter of Slippery Jim Fair thus uniting two substantial fortunes in what Mr. Dooley described as "gilt edge bonds of matrimony." The half million dollar pearls of Mrs. George Gould, who, a few years later would naturally ride the Western Pacific *(right)* stunned San Francisco. At the left, *The Overland* in 1900 and before an observation car was obligatory, rolls west at Evanston, Wyoming behind U.P. No. 1811. *(Wyoming State Historical Department.)*

Down the years and the decades they all rode *The Overland* and here are some of its notable patrons in the years between the wars: John Barrymore (1925) General John J. Pershing (1929) Paul Whiteman hamming it up with a striped trousered maitre d'hotel (1932) and Jackie Coogan (1923) on a baggage truck between his well upholstered parents whose pride and lordly source of income he was. (*Four Photos: Chicago Historical Society.*)

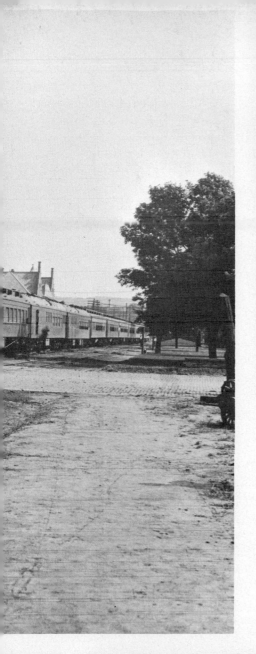

At the left *The Overland* pauses behind its Chicago & North Western's well groomed Pacific No. 1516 at Council Bluffs, Iowa, on a hot July morning in 1921 for its portrait by Homer O. Frohardt. Above: four years later it was only appropriate that "Miss California 1925" in the person of Miss Fay Lampier should head eastward aboard the train that more than any other symbolized The Golden State in the long legend of railroad travel. *(Left: William Kratville Collection; Above: Southern Pacific.)*

private and business cars of railroad officials, although by the fifties when it was running as a secondary train to *The City of San Francisco* it had become the ordinarily assigned train for company business cars and the private car *The Virginia City* owned by Charles Clegg and Lucius Beebe frequently rode at its rear end between Reno and Chicago or Oakland Mole. Another private varnish car often seen on Nos. 27 and 28 was *Laurel Ridge*, the ultra *moderne* company Pullman assigned to the conveniences of the President of United States Steel.

Mention has been made previously of the carriage of Adolphus Busch's private car eastbound in *The Overland* the night after the San Francisco fire and earthquake of 1906. The author has been able to unearth only one other instance in which private equipment was carried in its years as the crack train on the transcontinental run between Chicago and San Francisco.

The invaluable Merle Armitage recalls the occasion in 1919 when, as a special concession to the Muse Calliope, the Southern Pacific made an exception and took on the private car *General Stanley* which was the widely known conveyance of Ignace Jan Paderewski.

"Early in November of 1919 Paderewski cabled my partner and myself that he expected soon to resign as Premier of Poland and to return to his California property, an almond ranch at Paso Robles," recalls Mr. Armitage. "Because his Boston manager, the distinguished Charles A. Ellis was ill at the time, he requested that my partner and I book him four or five concerts on his way across the continent.

"This we were able to do on short notice because of the tremendous prestige and commanding popularity of this great musician and the *General Stanley* rolled smoothly between sold out houses in Cleveland, Chicago, Denver and Salt Lake City, at the last of which word was telephoned from San Francisco that the huge Municipal Auditorium had already sold 12,000 tickets and expected an audience of a capacity 15,000 two nights hence when we should arrive.

"We were attached to *The Pacific Limited* at Ogden, since *The Overland* in those days had a strictly enforced ruling against private cars and got to Reno on schedule. I was dining with Pade-

rewski while the car was in Reno yards when word was brought by the stationmaster that an unprecedented early December blizzard had collapsed a snow shed near Donner Summit and there would be 'some delay' in getting through.

"Well, any delay at all could be just about fatal and at this moment I saw through the window that *The Overland* which was still on the main line while we had been spotted on a passing track, showed every sign of impending departure, snow notwithstanding. It came to me that the Southern Pacific was going to make an all-out effort to get its candy train through while we waited for things to get organized on The Hill.

"I knew nobody personally in the upper S. P. echelons at the time but asked the Reno agent if I could use a company wire to call the general offices in San Francisco and was, using Pederewski's name as loudly and often as possible, shortly connected with the general manager's office. That august personage informed me that even the President of the U. S. didn't get his car on *The Overland* whereupon I explained as urgently as I could in polite terms, that 15,000 people were depending on the railroad to get an idolized performer to them and that if my principal didn't make an appearance next evening, San Franciscans would know it was because of official red tape and intransigence generally.

"We hung up on a note of mutual lack of cordiality and I feared the worst, but not more than 15 minutes later a switch engine took us off the end of *The Pacific Limited* and we were cut into *The Overland* between the mail cars and the first coach since *The Overland* in those times had its own observation car and nobody, not even God rode behind that.

"The episode ended on a happy note. We were all careful to see that the San Francisco papers were apprized of the special treatment and extra courtesy accorded the great pianist and a lot of good will was achieved by the S. P. management. But it gave me the worst 15 minutes of a career notable for shattering crises."

The decline of its affairs and position began for *The Overland* with the inaugural in the late thirties, if for brief periods only, of the luxurious extra fare *Treasure Island Special* and *Forty-Niner* for the duration of the San Francisco fair' and the gradual stepping up of service on *The City of San Francisco* from five times a month to the full time estate of a daily streamliner.

On borrowed time, it flourished mightily if not glitteringly through the war years following Pearl Harbor, its frequent second and occasional third sections pounding up the approaches to Sherman Summit within sight of each other in a density of wartime traffic that sometimes saw as many as forty train movements in a single day westward out of Omaha yards.

By the early fifties, however, the bloom was off railroad travel to such a melancholy degree that everywhere in the land services were being curtailed and once profitable name trains that had been national institutions suspended altogether. Perhaps the most calamitous of these was the consolidation by the once haughty Vanderbilt-owned New York Central of the *Commodore Vanderbilt* and *The Twentieth Century Limited* in 1957 and the downgrading of the hitherto all-Pullman extra fare *Century* to a train with daycoaches and no surcharge.

Attrition on *The Overland* was more gradual and manifested itself most notably on the Southern Pacific leg of its run. Diner service became demoralized and for a time it ran with a hamburger grill and then a coffee shop car between Oakland and Ogden. Sleeping cars remained well maintained to the very end, however, since they were not entirely under Southern Pacific jurisdiction and continued to run to Denver, Kansas City and St. Louis over the Union Pacific and Wabash long after it had ceased to be a through San Francisco to Chicago train.

In January of 1955 it gave up all pretentions of maintaining an Overland route schedule and carried, in addition to the Kansas City Pullmans only a single sleeping car and coach destined for Chicago. It remained as *The Overland* on the timecard of the Union Pacific as far as Omaha, but the name itself disappeared when its two through cars became part of the Chicago & North Western's Train No. 14 from there in.

The end of the proud *Overland Limited* as a daily train if not a through run to Chicago came on July 16, 1962, when the Interstate Commerce Commission finally authorized its suspension save at seasonal traffic peaks in June and December. The St. Louis cars became incorporated in *The City of San Francisco* and *The Overland* disappeared from the *The Official Guide* save between June 14 and Labor Day and from December 22 to January 2.

In a last despairing attempt to salvage at least the historic name, *The San Francisco Chronicle* waged a belated rear guard action to have the *Overland's* title bestowed on *The City of San Francisco. The City*, it pointed out editorially was of comparatively recent origin while *The Overland* had its roots in the immemorial past and was a part of the Old West in the dream world San Franciscans like to remember now as "Before The Fire." The name of *The Overland* was a cherished California heritage, it maintained, and its loss would be one more severed bond between the unsavory here and now and the good times gone.

High officialdom at 65 Market Street listened civilly and gave the matter its attention, but it pointed out, and not without justification, that *The City of San Francisco* was a name integrated over its connecting carriers with *The City of Los Angeles, City of Portland* and *City of St. Louis* and that the Union Pacific would take a dim view of breaking the pattern of its choicest name trains. Even if the Southern Pacific were amenable to calling it *The Overland* as far as Ogden, it was pointed out, it would inevitably become the *City of San Francisco* the moment it hit U. P. iron.

It is small consolation to its mourners that twice a year *The San Francisco Overland* is briefly revived in the public necessity and convenience. It is a ghost train on a stub run ending at Ogden and the continuity with the heroic past is broken forever.

But once in the glory days of its going it had been a blaze of wonderment and romance, the all-Pullman name train of classic pattern and matchless excellence. In its Palace Cars had ridden the great and powerful of earth and part of its perpetual lading had been the legend of splendor which it had created for itself. Let green attend its run down the long tangents of history and brightly glow its marker lamps in the gathering night of remembered things.

So far as the author has been able to discover, this is the first authenticated photograph of *The Overland Limited* after its recognition as a through name train by the Southern Pacific and its appearance in official company literature. It is shown double headed and presumably eastbound in one of the Sierra foothill depots with three head-end mail storage and R. P. O. cars and seven Pullmans behind two of the Espee's well maintained ten wheelers with characteristic wooden pilots, square steam chests and mammoth oil burning headlights. By now the candy train of its three connecting carriers, *The Overland* was established in the consciousness of the West and squared away for a long run into history. *(L. Jackson Welsh Collection.)*

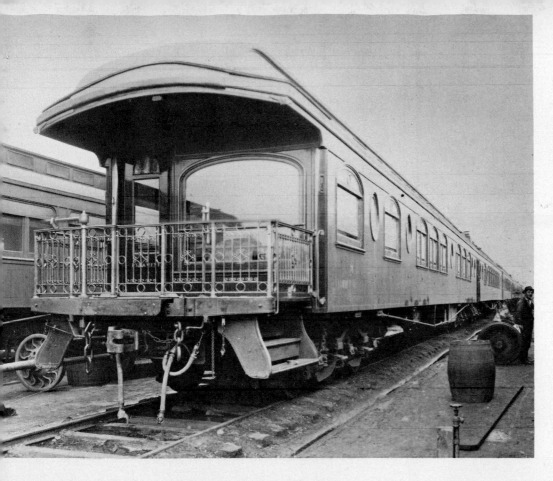

No record exists in the company archives of any Southern Pacific equipment specially built for service in the *Overland* pool of Pullmans such as was commissioned by both the Union Pacific and the North Western for this train. The observation-lounge car *Dynamene (left and below)* and the Espee diner *Castle Crags* shown on the transfer table at Sacramento were, however, typical of the splendid rolling stock that was assigned No. 1 and No. 2 shortly after the turn of the century. *(Left and Below: Arthur D. Dubin Collection; Bottom: D. L. Joslyn Collection.)*

The atmospheric midst reproduced above represents the interior of a Southern Pacific dining car of about 1899, the year *The Overland Limited* became a recognized and honored name west of Ogden. The derby was the universal traveling hat of masculine acceptance, the pork pie bonnet and severe shirtwaist its feminine counterpart. Mahogany woodwork was less intricately carved than it had been a decade earlier in the finest flowering of the Palace Car tradition, but chaste classic symmetry characterized transoms and ceilings and the possibility of failure in the new and largely experimental electric system was safeguarded by the presence of auxiliary and always reliable Pintsch gas lights. An Espee diner of this approximate period or slightly later is shown opposite, its wooden sheathing outmoded by the advent of steel construction and probably destined to end its days in maintenance of way service. The menu and wine card from the Palace Dining Car *Pacific*, date from an even earlier era on the Chicago & North Western where *Pacific* may well have been incorporated, as indeed its name suggests, in the first versions of the *Overland Flyer* on their run between Chicago and Council Bluffs. *(Above: Brown Bros.; Opposite, Top: Alfred W. Johnson Collection; Below: Southern Pacific.)*

PALACE DINING CAR PACIFIC.

DINNER.

Soup—Puree of Chicken

Fish—Baked White, Wine sauce

Boiled Leg of Mutton, Caper sauce

Rib Ends of Beef, browned Potatoes

Roast Beef   Turkey, Cranberry sauce
           Veal

Baked Pork and Beans

Lamb Pie, a la Anglaise
     Fillet of Beef, a la Jardiniere
                   Spanish Fritters

Chow Chow

Queen Olives   Celery
     Sweet Pickles

Boiled or Mashed Potatoes

Squash   Beets
    Green Corn   Green Peas

Suet Pudding, Brandy sauce

Pumpkin Pie   Apple Pie
     Cocoanut Charlotte

Edam Cheese   Bent's Crackers

Ice Cream   Assorted Cake

Fruit

Tea   Coffee

PRICE SEVENTY-FIVE CENTS.

PATRONS ARE AT LIBERTY TO RETAIN THIS BILL OF FARE AS A SOUVENIR.

WINE LIST.

CHAMPAGNE.

	Qts.	Pts.
Chapin & Gore's best, half pints, $1.00	$3 50	$2 00
G. H. Mumm's Extra Dry.	3 50	2 00
Piper Heidsick,	3 50	2 00
Pommery Sec,	3 50	2 00
Louis Roederer,	3 50	2 00
Arthur Roederer,	2 00	1 25
Cook's Imperial,	2 00	1 25

SAUTERNE.

Sauterne—Importation Speciale,	1 25	75
Latour Blanche,	2 00	1 25
Bellye Riesling, Hungarian,		75

CLARET.

Pontet Canet,	2 00	1 00
St. Julien, Imperial,	1 00	50
Finest Selected Hungarian,		75
Vin, Ordinaire (very good,)	hf pt. 15	

BROCTON (CHAUTAUQUA CO., N. Y.) WINES.

Sweet Catawba,	50
Dry Catawba,	50
Sunny Side,	50
Isabella,	50
Regina,	50
Claret,	50
Iona,	50

MISCELLANEOUS.

Amontillado Sherry, Superior,		1 00
Niersteiner Rhine Wine,	1 00	
Bass' Ale, White Label,		30
Guinness' Dublin Porter,		30
Belfast Ginger Ale,		25
Congress Water,		25
Apollinaris Water,		25
Hathorn Water,		25
Be-thes-da Water,		15
Budweiser Lager Beer,	30	20
Schlitz's Milwaukee Lager Beer,	30	15
Best's Milwaukee Lager Beer,	30	15
Whitney's Celebrated Crab Apple Cider,		25
Old Holland Gin,	hf. pt. flask,	50
Old Colcq, Pere & Fils Brandy,	" "	1 00
Old Consolation Rye Whisky,	Qts. 2 00 " "	50

Imported Cigars, very fine, 10, 15, 25 cts.   Cigarettes, bunch, 15 and 25 cts.

Be-thes-da Water furnished FREE to Guests of this Car.

NO WINES OR LIQUORS SOLD IN THE STATE OF IOWA

As splendid a train as any name flyer in the list was *The Overland Limited* as it posed for its portrait in 1905 with the train shed at Oakland Mole in the background. Its motive power was a high-

wheel it at high speeds as far as Sacramento but required a helper for the haul over The Hill. Conventional consist of the period was two head-end revenue cars, the classic *Overland* buffet, and

An early variation on the drumhead insigne of later usage was this modest electrically illuminated name box fixed to the observation platform railing to proclaim the passing of a proud train by day and by night. Below and at approximately the same period, Fred the smoke room steward attends the wants of patrons in a compartmented buffet car with a corridor separating the smoking compartment from a through passage. At the right, considerably later, perhaps about 1925, a matron conditions her offspring amidst the ample resources of the lady's retiring room. (*Left: Union Pacific; Below, Two Photos: Southern Pacific.*)

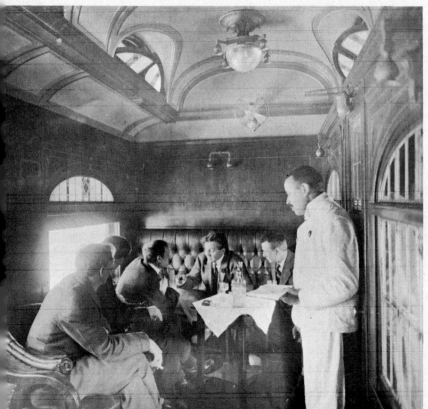

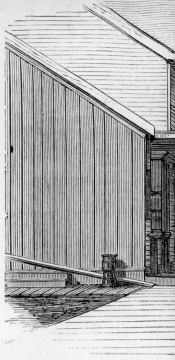

When in 1879, the drawing at the top of the opposite page was made, Elko wild and untamed and, as it still is, the center of Nevada cattle shipping was widely regarded as an outpost of Hell or Texas. When *The Overland's* secondary train, *The Pacific Limited*, double headed, paused there in 1905 things hadn't changed much, as witness the spirited scene reproduced above from *The Police Gazette* of September captioned: "Seeing Snakes For a Fact; Patrons of the Stockman's Saloon in Elko, Nevada, Found The Rattler was Real; The Management Had to Remove Him as a Detriment to Trade." The Pullman card (*below*) with cigarettes forbidden in Nevada, must date from one of the Silver State's brief but ineffectual skirmishes with morality. (*Photo: Wyoming State Historical Department.*)

For your comfort

OBSERVATION CAR

OUTDOOR platform, parlor for men and women, periodicals, newspapers, women's lounge and bath, maid in attendance

CLUB CAR FORWARD

BARBER, valet service, bath, lounge for smoking, periodicals, newspapers, market reports

Refreshing Drinks, Cigars and Cigarettes always available. Toilet articles may be purchased from barber.

A-1180 27·L. A. L.
REPRINT

No Cigarettes will be Sold from this Car while in Iowa, Utah or Nevada.

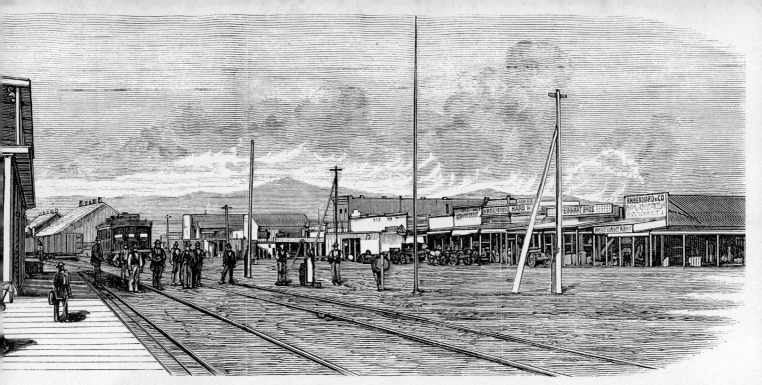

An elaborately printed hard cover souvenir book devoted to *The Overland Limited* copyrighted in 1897 and distributed to passengers with the compliments of the Union Pacific passenger department depicts in its full color illustrations Pullman equipment with both the Sissons Patent narrow vestibules and the full width vestibules of later practice, indicating that its components were of various ages. The buffet-smoking car combine, for example, had wide vestibules, the reclining chair coaches and diners had narrow. Both the diner *Aberlin* depicted on this page and *Wellington*, whose interior is below belonged in the Sissons category and derived from the early nineties. The colored reproduction of *Wellington* shows lavender drapes and portières, pale green ceilings and transoms with gold scrollwork and dark green leather upholstery. *(Three Photos: Pullman Standard.)*

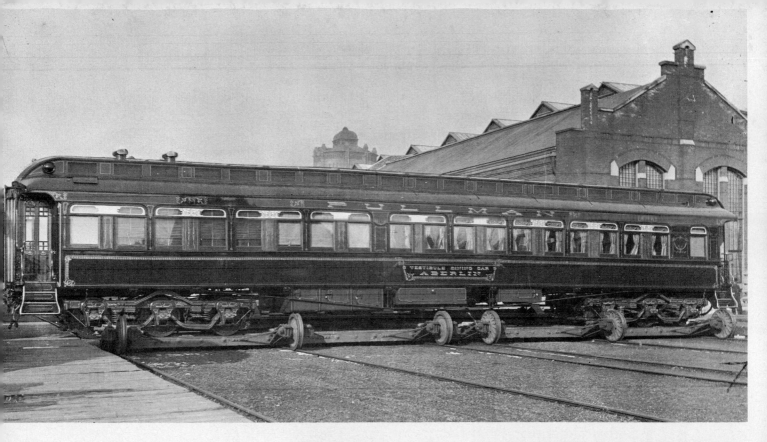

Although narrow vestibule equipment remained in service on the Overland run until approximately the turn of the century the Southern Pacific diner interior depicted below probably was photographed about 1910, if one may judge from the attire of the passengers. For many years the Espee serviced its Overland and Shasta trains from a bake shop adjacent to the great train shed at Oakland Mole and its diners were celebrated for their fresh bread and rolls and elaborate pastry. In the age of private cars, knowing owners invariably cautioned their stewards to put in a fresh supply from the Oakland bakery. The private car track was directly under the kitchen windows and, in an age innocent of air conditioning, the smell of fresh bread baking was irresistible. *(Southern Pacific.)*

The Overland Limited

ELECTRIC LIGHTED

The fastest, most complete and best equipped through transcontinental train, via the most direct route, less than three days San Francisco and Portland to Chicago, over the only double-track railway between the Missouri River and Chicago. All the provisions for comfort and luxury known to modern travel are included in its equipment.

The Best of Everything.

Three trains daily to Chicago, and two to St. Paul, Minneapolis and Duluth from Los Angeles, San Francisco and other California points, via the

Southern Pacific, Union Pacific
AND
Chicago & North-Western Rys.

Round-trip tourist tickets at reduced rates on sale daily. For tickets, sleeping car reservations and full information apply to Southern Pacific agents or address

R. R. RITCHIE,
Gen'l Agent Pacific Coast,
617 Market Street,
SAN FRANCISCO.

W. D. CAMPBELL,
Gen'l Agent,
247 South Spring Street,
LOS ANGELES.

W. A. COX,
Gen'l Agent,
153 Third Street,
PORTLAND, ORE.

Chicago & North-Western Railway

OLI42

Included in its portfolio of properties in 1905 along with resort hotels and vast real estate holdings was the Southern Pacific owned *Sunset Magazine*, a widely read West Coast monthly much of whose editorial energy was directed to promoting the fortunes of the railroad. One of *Sunset's* leading contributors earlier in the century, Paul Shoup became president of the company in 1929, although there is not necessarily any connection. In this house ad from *Sunset* in 1905 the electrically lighted *Overland Limited* was characterized as having "the best of everything." It did, too. (*Southern Pacific.*)

Named, not for the scene of Napoleon's exile but for a California resort community, the vestibuled Pullman Palace sleeping car *Santa Helena*, against a typical background of eucalyptus trees that lent its Sacramento shops a pastoral atmosphere, awaits minor repairs between runs. Regularly assigned to *The Overland Limited* until the narrow vestibule cars were replaced, *Santa Helena* was one of the cars on the Chicago run to become a household name, one with *Palmyra*, *Marlborough* and the diner *Pacific*. Tourist sleepers *(left)* were only a little less sumptuous than the Palace Cars and were identifiable principally by their rattan seats. On them gentlemen wore cutaway suits and ladies the flowered chapeaux later made famous by Queen Mary. *(Left: Southern Pacific; Below: David L. Joslyn.)*

In the illimitable reaches of the Nevada desert, *The Overland Limited* achieved its true dimension as a property of the Far West. Here its all-Pullman consist in the glory years established direct continuity with the legendary past, the Emigrant Trace that paralleled its route and the long *jornada* of death across the Humboldt Sink. Above at the left is shown the depot platform at Tracy, California, in 1907 with *The Owl* awaiting its Sacramento connection containing the Los Angeles sleeper indicated in the equipment schedule on this page. Above, and with its observation platform still innocent of identifying drumhead, *The Overland*, with two Southern Pacific engines on the head end for the Sierra grade, passes the Truckee River west of Reno. At the left, below, in the era of Pullman Standard in the mid-thirties *The Limited* passes on its lawful occasions near Elko, its going framed by twin semaphores against the Big Sky of the Nevada wasteland. *(Page Opposite, Two Photos: Southern Pacific; Above: Wyoming State Historical Department.)*

Via C. U. P. & N-W. Line. Daily.	
Lv Chicago	*•*6.00 pm
Lv Peoria	†5.30 pm
Ar Des Moines	*5.55 am
Ar Missouri Valley	7.10 am
Ar Sioux City	9.15 am
Ar Omaha	8.23 am
Ar North Platte (C.T.)	5.30 pm
Lv North Platte (M.T.)	4.35 pm
Ar Cheyenne	11.50 pm
Ar Green River	10.35 am
Lv Green River	10.40 am
Ar Ogden	4.50 pm
Ar Salt Lake	6.15 pm
Lv Ogden	5.10 pm
Ar Sparks (M.T.)	9.40 am
Lv Sparks (P.T.)	8.45 am
Ar Sacramento	4.50 pm
Ar Port Costa	7.00 pm
Ar San Francisco	8.28 pm
Lv Sacramento	5.15 pm
Ar Tracy	7.30 pm
Ar Fresno	11.05 pm
Ar Los Angeles (PT)	8.55 am
Lv Green River (M.T.)	10.50 am
Ar Pocatello	7.00 pm
Ar Butte	5.20 am
Ar Boise	3.45 am
Ar Huntington (M.T.)	6.00 am
Lv Huntington (P.T.)	5.10 am
Ar Pendleton	11.40 am
Ar Spokane	10.10 pm
Ar Portland (O.R. & N.)	8.20 pm

The Overland Limited, No. 1.

For first-class Sleeping Car passengers only. Electric Lighted train—electric reading lamps in each section and compartment.

A superb service of Pullman Standard Drawing Room and Private Compartment Sleeping Cars (electric reading lamp in each section and compartment) and Composite Observation Cars (with Buffet and Library) Chicago to San Francisco. Dining Cars, meals "a la carte." Connection at Cheyenne with Pullman Drawing Room Sleeping Car Denver via Cheyenne to Salt Lake City.

The San Francisco Sleeper connects via Sacramento at Tracy with "The Owl," having Pullman Drawing Room Sleeping Cars, Buffet Smoking and Library Cars San Francisco to Los Angeles via Fresno.

The "Coaster," with Observation Parlor Cars, Chair Cars and Dining Car, leaves San Francisco v*8.00 a. m. via Coast Division, arrives Los Angeles 11.15 p. m.

Pullman Standard Drawing Room and Private Compartment Sleeping Cars Chicago to Portland without change, connecting at Pocatello with Pullman Drawing Room Sleeping Cars from Salt Lake to Butte and Boise and connecting at Pendleton with Parlor Cafe Car Pendleton to Spokane.

See "Yellowstone Park Service" Table 4.

Tourist Sleeping Car (from Denver) Cheyenne to Portland.

Buffet Smoking and Library Car from Green River to Portland via Pocatello.

Free Reclining Chair Car Green River to Portland, connecting at Pocatello with Coaches from Salt Lake to Butte.

Dining Car service Chicago to San Francisco, Los Angeles and Portland; also from Denver to Cheyenne.

Pullman Standard Sleeping Car Chicago to Omaha and Chicago to Sioux City via Mo. Valley.

Observation Cafe Car, Parlor Car and Coaches Missouri Valley to Sioux City.

Electric Lighted. For first-class Sleeping Car passengers only.

Via C. U. P. & N-W. Line. Daily.	
Lv Los Angeles	5.00 pm
Lv Fresno	2.40 am
Lv San Francisco (PT)	10.00 am
Ar Sparks (P.T.)	8.55 am
Lv Salt Lake (M.T.)	12.35 pm
Lv Ogden	1.50 pm
Ar Green River (M.T.)	8.20 pm
Lv Portland (O.R. & N.)	8.30 am
Lv Spokane	6.00 am
Lv Pendleton (P.T.)	4.40 pm
Lv Huntington (M.T.)	1.15 am
Lv Butte	2.15 am
Lv Pocatello	11.50 am
Lv Green River	8.30 pm
Ar North Platte (M.T.)	12.30 pm
Ar Omaha (C.T.)	9.40 pm
Lv Omaha	10.00 pm
Ar Chicago	12.30 pm

The Overland Limited, No. 2.

A superb service of Pullman Standard Drawing Room and Private Compartment Sleeping Cars (electric reading lamp in each section and compartment) and Composite-Observation Cars (with Buffet and Library) San Francisco to Chicago. Dining Cars, meals "a la carte."

The "Coaster," with Observation Parlor Cars, Chair Cars, and Dining Car, leaves Los Angeles *8.00 a. m. via Coast Division, arrives San Francisco v11.15 p. m. Connection at Ogden with Pullman Drawing Room Sleeping Car from Salt Lake via Ogden and Cheyenne to Denver.

Pullman Drawing Room Sleeping Car from Los Angeles via Fresno to San Francisco.

Buffet Smoking and Library Car Los Angeles to San Francisco and from Portland to Green River.

Pullman Standard Drawing Room and Private Compartment Sleeping Cars Portland to Chicago without change, and Pullman Drawing Room Sleeping Car from Boise (via Nampa) to Salt Lake, connecting at Pocatello with Pullman Drawing Room Sleeping Cars from Butte via Pocatello to Salt Lake.

Parlor Cafe Car Spokane to Pendleton.

Tourist Sleeping Car Portland to Denver (see No. 4.).

Free Reclining Chair Cars Portland to Green River, connecting at Pocatello with Coaches Butte to Salt Lake.

Dining Car service Los Angeles, San Francisco and Portland to Chicago, and from Cheyenne to Denver.

In the winter of 1917 the camera of Fred Jukes, veteran boomer railroad man and a pioneer action photographer of trains, was waiting just east of Elko, Nevada, as *The Overland Limited* whistled out of town after a light fall of snow. One of the great railroad photographs of all time, it shows No. 2 with its classic consist of Railway Post Office car, combination baggage-buffet, two Pullman sleepers, a diner and observation lounge in a portrait of railroading in the grand manner.

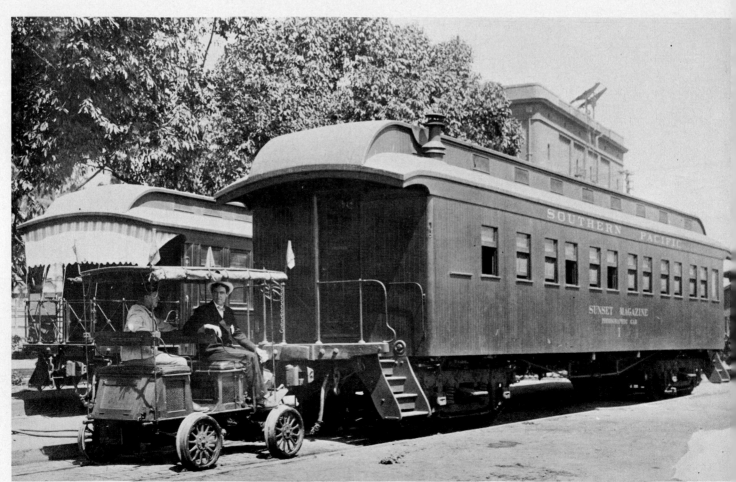

When in 1908 the Navy brought "The Great White Fleet" into San Francisco harbor and anchored off the Southern Pacific's then depot at Sixteenth Street *(opposite)* nobody had a better view of the scene than passengers on the eastbound *Overland Limited* and other crack trains leaving Oakland Mole. A very promotion minded railroad during the Harriman years, The Espee at that time published *Sunset Magazine* as what amounted to a house organ and its photographic dark room car and power scooters loaded with cameramen *(below)* went everywhere. While the fleet was in a staff photographer was inspired to take a view of *The Overland* as the carrier's crack train and hallmark of its prestige with the battleship *Iowa* for background, a timely photograph if ever there was one which received widespread publication and eventually sold more than a million copies as a postcard. *(Three Photos: Southern Pacific.)*

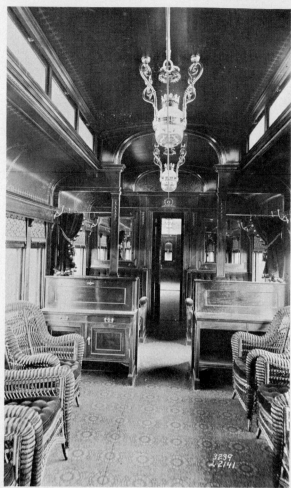

A companion piece, taken in more clement season, to another action shot of *The Overland Limited* leaving Elko, Nevada, by Fred Jukes and shown elsewhere in this volume is this springtime pastoral when the snows of winter have vanished but there is still sufficient chill in the desert air to show condensation of steam exhaust. The high wheeled Pacific with burnished tires, the turtle-back head-end equipment, all are implicit of the heritage of Harriman Standard which still governed passenger operations on the Southern Pacific in the year 1917. On the opposite page are the interiors of two combination baggage-buffet cars by Pullman, the one represented in the two top photographs dates from the turn of the century when Pintsch illumination was still almost universal, that below embodies the first electric lamps in the form of glazed bulbs in tulip-shaped electroliers. (*Above: Fred Jukes; Opposite, Three Photos: Pullman Standard.*)

When it was built and placed in service in 1879 to carry Central Pacific trains across the Straits of Carquinez between Benicia and Port Costa, the *Solano*, shown at the top of the opposite page with components of *The Overland* on board, was the largest train ferry in the world. Its two vertical beam engines of 1500 horsepower each and paddle wheels thirty feet in diameter were among the wonders of the engineering world and the brief water trip, like the even more spectacular ride across San Francisco Bay, was among the enjoyable interludes of the trip across the continent. From 1914 until the construction of the present bridge between Martinez and Benicia, the *Solano* was supplemented by the even larger *Contra Costa (below)* in handling the ever growing density of traffic between San Francisco and the north and east. During a given year, 1927, the two ferries carried the amazing total of 98,262 passenger cars and 148,130 freight cars without accident to equipment or personnel. The routing of trains, many of them crack limiteds on close schedules as well as perishable merchandise, through this bottleneck was a remarkable feat of logistics. Here *The Overland* double headed climbs the Sierra eastbound near Colfax about 1912. *(Opposite, Two photos: Southern Pacific; Above: Fred Jukes.)*

Although Apperson Jack Rabbits, Pope Hartfords and other vintage cars had appeared in the Nevada desert as far back as 1905 when they swarmed to the excitements at Tonopah, Goldfield and Bullfrog, only a single two seater with a "one man top" was visible in the main street of Elko when *The Limited* pulled in in 1916. At the right is a great storm lantern that had spread its coal oil illumination over the Southern Pacific depot platform at Reno when the railroad was new. In its uncertain light, the Comstock Kings had changed cars to board the Virginia & Truckee in bonanza times, and it had resisted the elements down the years to come to final rest in Virginia City's As It Was Museum. *(Top: Fred Jukes; Below: Mrs. Victor Maxwell.)*

At the turn of the century the accepted uniform of his exalted calling for a Southern Pacific conductor aboard *The Overland Limited* was a dark blue morning tailcoat, gold Albert watch chain to moor his Hamilton railroad watch and a fresh flower in the lapel. It was an age when old time travelers still addressed the conductor as "Captain" and to order the affairs of a name limited was a very prestigious occupation indeed. *(Southern Pacific.)*

Beginning in 1913, the secondary run to *The Overland* was made by trains No. 19-20, *The Pacific Limited* via the Southern Pacific and U.P. to Omaha, where it finished its trip into Chicago over the Milwaukee as *The Overland* itself had briefly done back in 1905. Although on a seventy-two and three-quarters hour schedule and carrying no surcharge, *The Pacific Limited* was comparatively luxurious but without the barber, valet, lady's maid and stenographer of *The Overland*. It is shown on the opposite page double headed out of Elko, Nevada, in 1916 in an action shot by Fred Jukes. At the right is a Pullman-built buffet assigned in 1915 to the San Francisco run while *(below)* in the depot at Davis, California, the two trains shared billing on the wall. A Sacramento grade crossing of the same year *(opposite)* was guarded by a uniformed watchman. *(Right: Pullman Standard; Below: Southern Pacific.)*

So great was the press of transcontinental traffic in the mid-twenties that, taking a leaf from the New York Central where an *Advance Twentieth Century Limited* was taking the pressure off Trains No. 25 and 26, the component railroads involved in the Overland run to San Francisco came up with an *Advance San Francisco Overland Limited*. Running on an almost precisely similar schedule to that of the regular *Overland* as Trains No. 29 and 30, *The Advance Overland* is shown on these two pages in its progress across Nevada. Above, double headed it swings around the long curve at Wells, while at the right Pullman passengers board No. 30 at Reno. Opposite it at the top the observation car is framed by signals at Carlin while below it makes time at Golconda. *(Four Photos: Southern Pacific.)*

Supplementing the principal source of supply in the galley area, a service bar in *The Virginia City's* main salon contained all essentials to survival including running water, refrigeration with room for a case or so of bottles.

The last private car maintained by non-railroad owners to claim the Southern Pacific for its home railroad, that is to say the originating carrier where it was stored when not in use, was the Pullman-built *Virginia City*, property of Charles Clegg and Lucius Beebe of Virginia City, Nevada. Of Pullman-Standard, all-steel construction and decorated by Robert Hanley of Hollywood in Venetian renaissance baroque, *The Virginia City* slept six in master bedrooms, seated eight at table and carried a crew of two. The owners maintained a parking track of their own at Pacific Grove on Monterey Peninsula for winter trips and occupied conventional private car tracks at such terminals as Miami, New Orleans, Jersey City, St. Louis and Seattle. At the top opposite is a group aboard it at dinner at Pacific Grove and next a view of the main salon showing its working fireplace of Venetian marble. Below is Chef Charlie Yee in his galley and the car spotted at West Palm Beach with A Florida East Coast engine standing by to maintain service connections. As long as *The Overland* remained on the operating timecards of the Southern Pacific and its U.P. connection, it was favored by the owners of *The Virginia City* when their occasions of business or pleasure took them east over a mid-continental routing. (*Interiors: Maynard Parker; Upper Left:* THE MONTEREY HERALD; *Left:* THE MIAMI HERALD.)

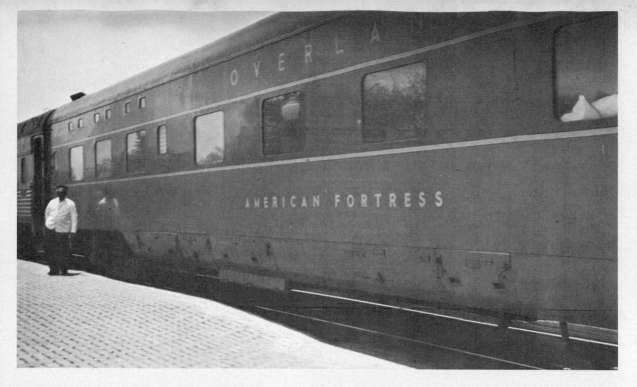

In its closing years as a through transcontinental name train, *The San Francisco Overland* still made a fine picture as it rolled behind one of the Southern Pacific's characteristic cab-first articulated locomotives eastbound through the Sierra foothills at twilight. One of its sleepers that still carried the radiant name *Overland* on its nameboards was *American Fortress, (opposite)* and in summer it was still daylight when the brakeman got down to flag at Roseville. *(Opposite, Top: Douglas C. Wornom; Below: Philip Hastings; Above: Southern Pacific.)*

In 1926 when fifty-one trains a day were listed for departure from Oakland Mole, *The San Francisco Overland Limited* departed at 11:30 a.m., today from Track 10, to be followed at a two hour interval by the *St. Louis Express*, and *The Overland* was still the candy train of the transcontinental run. A quarter of a century later when it is depicted opposite leaving Truckee behind a cab-first articulated, its prestige had declined and head-end revenue was much in evidence, but it still made a handsome portrait. *(Opposite: Jim Ady; Below: Southern Pacific.)*

By 1957 No. 27 was reduced on the Union Pacific leg of its run to the estate of a mail and express train with ten cars of head-end revenue and two rider coaches where once the Pullmans had ridden in glory. On the Southern Pacific run from Oakland to Ogden (left) the *Overland* still was characterized by the newest thing in coaches and streamlined sleepers for Denver and St. Louis right up to the end of its life. (*Above: Richard Kindig; Left: Lucius Beebe.*)

Back in 1916 when Fred Jukes caught *The Overland Limited* in classic pose of action on the Southern Pacific at Elko, Nevada, behind No. 2404, the Espee was advertising it as "The Aristocrat" of trains and it was indeed the finest thing on wheels west of the Mississippi. *(Above: Fred Jukes; Left: Grahame Hardy Collection.)*

The Overland and *The Gold Coast* were still among the living when the photograph below was taken of the train board at Oakland Mole in the early fifties but the list was sadly abated from the time a few years before when fifty trains a day departed the long gloomy train shed at the end of the ferry ride. In the last months of its regularly scheduled existence, however, as suggested opposite *The Overland* was never demeaned by the devices of shabby equipment or shiftless operations, and day coaches and Pullmans were of the newest streamlined design and beautifully maintained on the run to Ogden where its St. Louis sleepers were integrated to the Union Pacific's *City of St. Louis*, a train of great style. *(Below: Richard Steinheimer; Opposite, Top: Lucius Beebe; Below, Two Photos: Philip R. Hastings.)*

MINORS MUST NOT PLAY

The San Francisco Overland, while it was still a first class train on the Southern Pacific whose elements were absorbed in other trains by the U. P. at Ogden, is shown at the left in the High Sierra running five hours late during the exceptionally inclement winter of 1962, its Diesel exhaust muted against the snow-covered ballast. In more auspicious weather the progress of No. 28 is depicted in a series of vignettes along the top of the page representing the waiting room of the depot at Sacramento where travelers waited under a mural depicting Leland Stanford turning the first spade in the construction of the Central Pacific in 1863, the rear brakeman in conversation on the platform at Sacramento, and, at the extreme right, its cars engulfed in one of the Sierra snowsheds of wintry aspect more in keeping with the picture at the left. *(Left: Richard Steinheimer; Above, Three Photos: Philip R. Hastings.)*

In the last year of its regularly scheduled operation on a year 'round basis, *The San Francisco Overland* still made a Christmas card picture in a Sierra snowstorm. Although it carried only a diner, two coaches and the Denver, Kansas City and St. Louis sleepers (the Salt Lake Pullman had disappeared a few years before) on the day it was photographed in the winter of 1962 by Richard Steinheimer, it carried an enclosed solarium club car on its rear end. At Ogden its components were absorbed by the Union Pacific's *City of St. Louis* and its head end revenue cars continued as Trains 27 and 28 between Ogden and Omaha with only a rider coach as passenger accommodations.

In 1897 when this photograph was posed on the great Dale Creek Trestle, the second such structure to span this deep abyss near Sherman Summit in Wyoming, company literature attests that both Pullman and Wagner sleeping cars were used interchangeably in *The Overland Limited.* Viewed under a reading glass the fourth and fifth cars, both sleepers, in the photograph at the right reveal the legend "Wagner" on their nameboards while the combination buffet and baggage car ahead of them is merely marked "Union Pacific" although its window arrangement and structural design strongly suggest that it, too, was a product of Pullman's most resolute competition. The Chicago & North Western, on whose lines *The Overland* originated at Chicago was a Vanderbilt property at the time and Vanderbilt roads patronized Webster Wagner exclusively for luxury equipment. Two years later Wagner was absorbed by Pullman and disappeared from the lexicon of travel. Sketch artists never tired of Dale Creek as is suggested by the engraving from *Leslie's* twenty years earlier. Wagner sleepers *(above)* displayed craftsmanship fully as meticulous as Pullman and somewhat more ornate. The Wagner hallmark was the little collonade of beautifully turned onyx pillars at the far end of the clerestory. *(Above: Pullman Standard; Right: Ewing Galloway.)*

In 1887 when the first *Overland* started west, the trains of the North Western, Burlington and Rock Island converged at Council Bluffs, shown at the bottom opposite, and passengers changed to the Union Pacific to cross the Missouri on the long bridge, shown in the photograph and line drawing, to depart from the U.P. depot in the center. U.P. American Standard 4-4-0 engines such as No. 711 powered both freight and passenger runs of the time, and mails for points east and west were still sometimes exchanged on the Great Plains as depicted below. *(Photo Opposite: American Geographical Society; Above: Richard H. Kindig Collection.)*

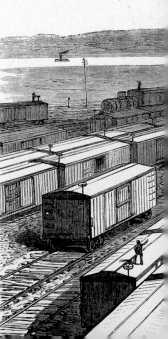

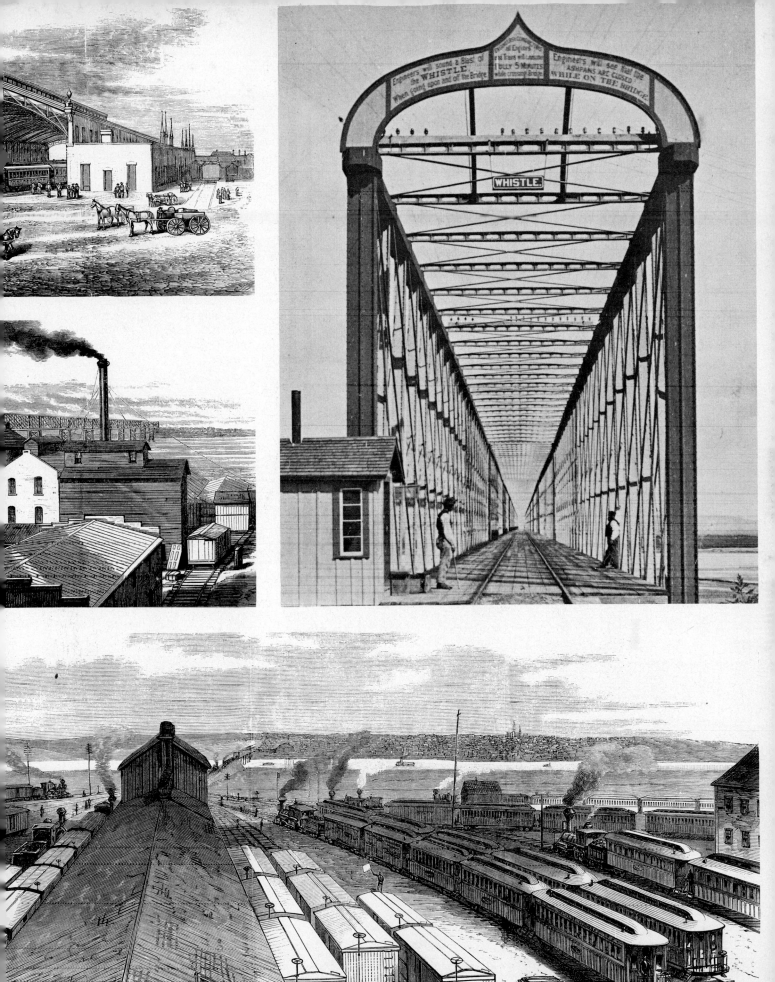

Connecting at Grand Junction with the Denver & Rio Grande Railroad and the Colorado Midland Railway.

Ogden to Denver.			Trains Run Daily.		Denver to Ogden.	
Atlantic Express.	Fast Mail.	Miles	‖ Meals. ☊ Telegraph Office. Mountain Time:	Elev.	Fast Mail.	Pacific Express.
7 00AM	6 00PM	0	lv..**San Francisco**..ar	14	9 45AM	6 45AM
7 20PM	7 00AM	0	lv.....**Ogden**.....☊ar	4340	1 00AM	2 30PM
8 25 "	8 05 "	37	.....Salt Lake	4227	11 59PM	1 30PM
9 35 "	9 26 "	82	........Provo...	4517	10 17 "	11 55AM
12 10AM	11 55AM	134	..Pleasant Valley Jct	7177	7 55 "	9 30 "
3 10 "	3 10PM	223	.....Green River	4369	4 10 "	5 25 "
‖6 15PM	‖6 15PM	325	ar...**Grand Junc**...☊	4583	1 00PM	2 10AM
6 35AM	6 35PM	325	lv...**Grand Junc**..☊ar	4583	‖12 40PM	1 40AM
8 45AM	8 38PM	402	....Newcastle....☊	....	10 25AM	10 20PM
1 19PM	1 01AM	506	...Leadville ...☊	10200	5 50 "	6 50 "
‖3 23 "	3 05 "	564	.....Salida....☊	7050	3 15 "	4 20 "
5 05 "	4 51 "	620	....Canon City...☊	5344	1 02AM	2 08 "
6 45 "	6 30 "	661	....**Pueblo**....☊	4699	11 40PM	‖12 50PM
8 04 "	7 56 "	706	.Colorado Springs.☊	5992	10 20 "	11 20AM
10 30PM	10 30AM	781	ar....**Denver**....☊lv	5196	7 30PM	8 30AM
6 25AM		346	lv... **Grand Junc**..☊ar	4583		1 45AM
8 25 "		423	....Newcastle....☊	...		11 20PM
‖10 00AM		459	Aspen Junction...☊			‖9 17 "
‖1 25PM		521	...Leadville ...☊	....		5 50PM
7 30 "		657	.Colorado Springs.☊	5992		11 10AM
11 00PM		731	ar....**Denver**..☊lv	5197		8 35AM

Shown above in an excerpt from the Southern Pacific's Ogden Route timetable for 1895 showing the Atlantic *and* Pacific Express *connections with the Denver & Rio Grande and Colorado Midland at Ogden. These through cars for Denver were carried in* The Overland *after its acceptance by the Espee in 1899. (Southern Pacific.)*

From the beginning of its importance as a railroad town when the Union Pacific-Central Pacific interchange removed there from Promontory, Ogden was predominantly a U.P. protectorate. In 1887 when the first Union Pacific version of *The Overland Limited* paused there, it had changed little in appearance from its look of eighteen years earlier when A. J. Russell took the photograph below. Ogden was a cow town, market town, railroad town of false fronts and unpaved streets and passengers who descended from the Pullmans were entirely aware that they were in an outpost of the Old West. They knew it in equal measure all the way across Nevada when the Lucin Cut-off was still in the future and trains took the long way around the north end of Great Salt Lake. At the top opposite, passengers are shown about 1900 boarding the Colorado Midland connecting train at Ogden, while below, in 1908, *The Overland Limited* speeds westbound through Morgan, Utah, while a long fruitblock occupies the eastbound iron. The tracks occupy essentially the same positions today. *(Below: American Geographical Society; Opposite: Colorado College Library, Wyoming State Historical Department.)*

In the bright noontide of its enviable going, *The Overland Limited*, shown here at Rock Springs, Wyoming, behind Union Pacific No. 1849 with wooden pilot beam and cowcatcher, was a household name throughout the American continent. To ride it in the company of Mme. Emma Nevada or John Mackay, perhaps with Edward H. Harriman's private car *Arden* at the end of its consist, was a status symbol long before Madison Avenue coined the phrase. In the lexicon of name trains it was the peer of *The Twentieth Century Limited*, the Milwaukee's *Pioneer Limited* and *The Merchants'* on the New Haven, which was to be at the very summit of desirability. The diner and buffet whose interiors are depicted opposite are from the same period, circa 1905. *(Above: Wyoming State Historical Department; Opposite, Above: Southern Pacific; Below: Union Pacific.)*

In *The Overland's* spacious times, as was the case aboard any extra-fare transcontinental, all the amenities of a metropolitan hotel were taken for granted in the form of restaurants, bars, barber shops and their allied and complementary services. At the bottom of the opposite page *The Overland* is shown on the Union Pacific at Lane Cut-off in 1908 while above are interiors of the barber shop and a lady's washroom of approximately the same period. The manicure scene and service tariffs on this page date from a somewhat later period, about 1926. *(Opposite, Below: Wyoming State Historical Department; Above, Pullman Standard; Here, Two Pictures: Grahame Hardy Collection.)*

OBSERVATION-CLUB CAR

Barber, valet service, bath, writing desk, periodicals, newspapers, market reports. Lounge for smoking.

Barber Shop

(Observation-Club Car)

Men

Hair Cut	.50
Shave	.25
Beard Trimmed	.35
Hair Singe	.25
Facial Massage	.50
Facial Massage (Boncilla)	1.00
Plain Shampoo	.50
Shampoo, Egg, Oil or Tonic	.75
Hair Tonics	.25
Bath	.50

Women

Hair Bob	.75
Hair Bob—Trim	.50
Neck Clip	.25
Plain Shampoo	1.00
Shampoo, Egg, Oil or Tonic	1.25
Hair Tonics	.25
Bath (Maid will arrange)	.50

VALET SERVICE

(Observation-Club Car)

Trousers (Pressing)	.35
Vest	.25
Coat	.65
Suit	1.00
Overcoat	1.00
Woman's Coat	1.00
Woman's Suit	1.25
Woman's Skirt	.75

Valet service from 6:30 in the morning to midnight The porter of the sleeping car will arrange for this service. Please advise at what hour you desire to have clothes returned.

Ladies' Maid

Skilled in manicuring, hair dressing and other personal services.

Manicuring	.75
Hairdressing	.75

Dining Car

Between Chicago, San Francisco and Los Angeles. A la carte service.

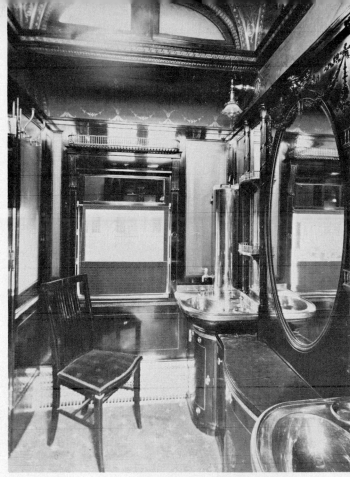

When, in 1906, *The Overland Limited* got its highball out of Rawlins *(opposite)* the engineer cleared his cylinder cocks in one of the bravura gestures incidental to whistling off in steam for a fine portrait by Fred Jukes. In the photograph on this page showing the nicely maintained depot lawn that was a Union Pacific feature for many years, the same turreted and gabled structure appears on the far side of Rawlins' main street. Laramie station *(below)* was a far more imposing structure than it is today. *(Opposite: Fred Jukes; Above and Below: Wyoming State Historical Department.)*

As an indication of the success of *The Overland Limited* as a de luxe flyer on the Chicago-California run, it is notable that a new companion train, *The Los Angeles Limited* was inaugurated in January 1906 following the route of *The Overland* as far as Ogden where it diverged toward Southern California over the rails of Senator William Andrews Clark's Los Angeles & Salt Lake line. *The Los Angeles Limited*, depicted here on its maiden run in a photograph by J. E. Stimson of Cheyenne somewhere in the Utah desert south of Salt Lake City, was not all-Pullman but provided chair cars over the Chicago & North Western as far as Omaha and both Standard Pullmans and tourist sleepers through to Los Angeles. Its observation lounge cars were specially assigned equipment and bore the train's name on sideboards and in a sort of primeval illuminated drumhead above the observation platform. This special Pullman equipment was interchangeable and sometimes ran in *The Overland* as is testified in another photograph by Stimson showing *The Overland* running beside the Humboldt on the Southern Pacific with a *Los Angeles Limited* observation car in its consist. The Union Pacific, over whose rails the new train was soon to run all the way from Omaha to the Pacific, emphasized its character as a companion to *The Overland* in its advertising and promotional literature. *(Above: Union Pacific; Right: Wyoming State Historical Department.)*

This is the look of Dale Creek a few miles west of Sherman Summit immediately after the famous spidery Dale Creek Trestle which for years had been a landmark for the westward landfarer had been replaced by a solid fill in the same location as is occupied by the more substantial fill which carries the mainline today. The train posed in the photograph, as is suggested by the personnel on the cars' steps and on the fillside despite the wind-born exhaust, is identified by the photographer as Train No. 5, *The California & Oregon Express*, westbound, some of whose Pullmans will be cut out at Green River for the Portland cutoff at Granger while the rest of the train continues to its Southern Pacific connection at Ogden. *(Wyoming State Historical Department.)*

In the years before the coming of identifying train insignes on the observation platform, *The Overland Limited* heads east out of Cheyenne towards its rendezvous with the North Western at Omaha. (*Wyoming State Historical Department.*)

Just as it is the time-honored custom among the captains of Atlantic liners upon occasion to comment that their most recent was "the stormiest crossing within memory," so veteran railroaders on the Great Plains went on record that the winter of 1916-17 transcended in ferocity anything within recollection. The clipping at the right from *The Laramie Republican* of Tuesday, December 19, 1916, details a wreck of *The Overland Limited* and the presence on the scene of William M. Jeffers, then General Manager, later President of the Union Pacific. At the top opposite, later that winter an *Overland* diner is thawed out at Laramie after three days in a snowdrift to the west. Below, a rotary clears a passage at Rock Springs after the same storm that immobilized the diner. The line drawing, made twenty-five years earlier, shows that winter on the Wyoming rails had been a favorite of periodical artists even before the turn of the century. (*Two Photos & Clipping: Wyoming State Historical Collection.*)

WRECKED IN STORM

SNOW PLOW CRASHES INTO OBSERVATION CAR OF OVERLAND LIMITED PASSENGER TRAIN AT LOOKOUT IN NIGHT

One of Worst Snow Storms in History of Railroad Encountered at Midnight, Engineers Being Unable to See Ahead—One Brakeman Injured When Engine Collides With Caboose in Yards at Hanna.

A disastrous wreck occurred near Lookout at about 1 o'clock this morning, when a snow plow ran into the rear of the observation car of train No. 1, the Overland Limited, one of the finest trains in the west and the finest on the Union Pacific, fortunately no one being hurt. The car was demolished and the snow plow was put out of commission.

The lateness of the hour for the rear end collision at Lookout, at which time the observation car was empty, made the injuries of no consequence. The observation car was almost on top of the snow plow, and the cars were so tightly wedged together that it took some time to pull them apart. The track was blocked for several hours.

Country's Worst Storm.

Trainmen state that the storm at and around Lookout last night was one of the worst ever experienced there, rendering the operation of trains very difficult. From the reports received here, a freight train just ahead of the Overland Limited was stalled in the snow, and No. 1 was compelled to stop for the freight. The snow plow, coming right behind, could not see the passenger train in time to avoid the collision, the wreck resulting.

General Manager W. M. Jeffers, who was in his official car attached to train No. 9, left his car here and hastened to the scene of the wreck on No. 17, and was in charge of the clearing of the track. He was joined later by Superintendent Bell, Assistant Superintendent Woodruff and other officials of the division. The trains from the west used the eastbound track and there was little delay on account of the wreck.

At the right is Omaha Union Station in a time when no automobile showed on the overpass across the tracks while below, *The Overland Limited* heads westward in 1907 under the famed image of the buffalo head on the long bridge between Council Bluffs and Omaha. *(Three Photos: Wyoming State Historical Department.)*

The original iron bridge across the Missouri River between Council Bluffs and Omaha and serving the Union Pacific is depicted on previous pages and lasted until 1888 when ever increasing traffic necessitated a double track structure capable of sustaining vastly heavier loads than its predecessor. The double tracked span shown on these pages went into service when *The Overland Limited* was a a year old and lasted until 1916 when it was again replaced by the even more structurally satisfactory span in use to this day. The huge copper buffalo head that ornamented the highest girder at the Council Bluffs end of the bridge symbolized the West and faced eastward, so that it was seen to best advantage by occupants of the observation platforms of trains that had already been where the deer and the buffalo roamed. The massive ornament which contained 3,000 pounds of copper, tin and zinc and was mounted on a 1,000 pound iron frame, was suggested by Charles Francis Adams who was President of Union Pacific when the second bridge was built. Under it passed *The Overland Limited* for fifty-four years before it became a victim of wartime hysteria in 1942 and was melted down for scrap. Legend holds that Adams was so revolted by the slaughter of the Great Plains buffalo, many of which, in the railroad's early days, had been shot from moving trains, that he ordered the buffalo head as a memorial token until the super-patriots got their hands on it. At the other end of the bridge was a bronze bas-relief depicting a plow, anchor and steam jackhammer, presumably symbols of progress. It was held in low esteem by the artistically inclined.

A division point of major importance in early days of transcontinental traffic and one where for many years cars were cut out of California-bound varnish runs for inclusion in Portland trains diverging from the main line a few miles west at Granger, Green River, Wyoming, was very much a railroading town until the advent of Diesel. Its identifying butte which shows in all three of the illustrations on these pages was and is a permanent feature of the Wyoming landscape, but for fully half the years of the railroad's existence an almost equally satisfying landmark was the ornate premises with battlements and crenalated towers of the Green River Brewery just across the Union Pacific's well kept depot lawn. At the right is Green River as it appeared to a sketch artist from *Leslie's Weekly* in 1876, while above is a beautifully maintained U. P. ten wheeler photographed just before the turn of the century by the veteran Fred Jukes. On this page in a rare photograph dating from the late seventies is what appears to have been a particularly exotic version of highball signal located at the depot platform. The ball itself, *page 114* visible and blurred, apparently was hoisted on halyards into a pentagonal housing when not displaying a clear track. *(Opposite, Top: Fred Jukes; Above: Wyoming State Historical Department.)*

Although still sternly rejected by the Southern Pacific, *The Overland* was the featured train in the joint Union Pacific-Chicago & North Western timetable for 1897 whose back cover is reproduced on the page opposite. Here it is shown in 1905 crossing Hanna Forks Bridge at Granger, Wyoming, in its all-Pullman glory when the fine sleeper *Bernardino* and the U.P. Buffet No. 711 carried its name on specially assigned luxury equipment. *(Above: Wyoming State Historical Department; Below and Opposite: A. W. Johnson Collection.)*

In an older lexicon of railroading train orders picked up along the way were often known as "the staff" and the reason is demonstrated in this photograph dating from the first decade of the century from the Wyoming State Archives at Cheyenne. It is captioned *The Overland* Picking up the *Staff* at Buford," and in a time before the wicker hoops and butterflies of a later usage the orders were protected from the elements in a metal tube much like those used in pneumatic communications systems in large stores. The staff was looped to an arm within easy reach of the cab window which was fitted with a lantern to indicate an order board at night. In an uncomplicated age of railroading, picking up the staff was a commonplace and part of the everyday experience of train crews everywhere. *(Wyoming State Historical Department.)*

The coal tipple at Wamsutta, Wyoming, and the water plug at Sidney, Nebraska, with its lantern to show its position at night were the familiar facilities for fueling the iron horse at the turn of the century. *(Two Photos; Wyoming State Historical Department.)*

In addition to its Pacific Coast destinations, *The Over-land* in 1897 maintained a Denver section with reclining chair cars, Standard sleepers, diners and observation lounge cars which left Denver at 10:30 in the evening and operated as a separate train via Julesburg to Omaha where it arrived at 4:45 the next afternoon. From Omaha to Chicago the Denver cars were a part of No. 2 arriving at 7:45 the following morning. Train No. 3, in actual fact the westbound Denver section of

The Overland, shown above rolling into Denver yards a few years after the above date, was listed as *The Fast Mail.* At the top of the opposite page the *Denver Over-land* eastbound pauses on a summer morning at Julesburg; below, it is made up in Denver Union Station, easily identified by the clock tower and tracks laid for both standard and narrow gauge operations. *(Three Photos: Wyoming State Historical Department.)*

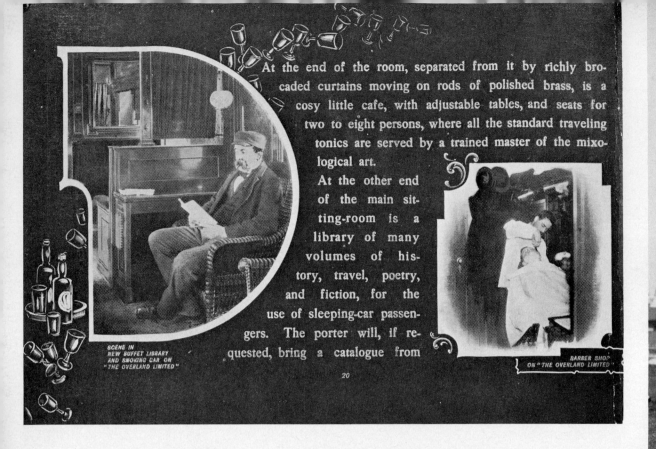

At the end of the room, separated from it by richly brocaded curtains moving on rods of polished brass, is a cosy little cafe, with adjustable tables, and seats for two to eight persons, where all the standard traveling tonics are served by a trained master of the mixological art.

At the other end of the main sitting-room is a library of many volumes of history, travel, poetry, and fiction, for the use of sleeping-car passengers. The porter will, if requested, bring a catalogue from

SCENE IN
NEW BUFFET LIBRARY
AND SMOKING CAR ON
"THE OVERLAND LIMITED"

BARBER SHOP
ON "THE OVERLAND LIMITED"

20

An enchanting insight into the look and feeling of railroad travel at the turn of the century may be had from the pages of an elaborate advertising brochure published by the Union Pacific in 1901 and devoted to hymning the wonders of the new equipment of *The Overland Limited*. Two pages from it are reproduced here to suggest that well upholstered comfort was the dominant characteristic of transcontinental travel when McKinley the Good was in the White House. (*Two Photos: Union Pacific.*)

pipes in the car are filled with water, and heated by live steam from a jacket through which steam passes, causing hot water to circulate, giving uniform heat.

PERFECT
CAR ILLUMINATION.

Among other luxuries and conveniences on this train will be found perfect car illumination — Pintsch light, so called from the name of its discoverer, Julius Pintsch, of Berlin. This mode of lighting is the only absolutely safe method at present in existence, and

SCENE IN DINING CAR ON "THE OVERLAND LIMITED"

24

On its old schedule *The Overland* arrived at Evanston, Wyoming, eastbound, at 11:15 on a summer's morning just as the sun was nearing the yardarm as is indicated by the shadows of the trees on its neatly maintained depot lawn. In all probability it had been double headed for the long grade up Weber and Echo Canyons and the helper engine had been uncoupled before Photographer Stimson took this atmospheric shot with No. 123 for the road. At the left is the station platform farther east at Hanna, Wyoming, where an eastbound train, probably not *The Overland* from its consist, paused for coal and water fuel while passengers got down from the cars to take the air. (*Two Photos: Wyoming State Historical Department.*)

The Harriman program of rehabilitation of the entire plant of the Union Pacific was in full operation when *The Overland*, westbound behind No. 1805, was photographed in 1904 drifting downgrade in Fish Cut, Utah, where the roadbed had only recently been double-tracked. At the left the same train is depicted where the canyon walls close in on either side only a few miles east of Ogden, the smoke that envelopes the Pullmans being, not engine exhaust, but from brakeshoes overheated on the steep descent to the level of Salt Lake Valley. *(Two Photos: Wyoming State Historical Department.)*

The long descent through Echo and Weber Canyons from Wahsatch to the junction with the Southern Pacific at Ogden finds the Union Pacific right of way passing through stupendous geologic formations, many of which were given suggestive names by the pioneers, Mormons and later surveyors for the railroad, who first encountered them. There are Castle Rock, Monument Rock, the Devil's Slide, Steamboat Rocks and The Narrows. Here *The Overland* westbound in 1907 or 1908, its beautifully proportioned observation lounge still innocent of identifying insigne but carrying green to signify a following section, passes beneath the shaggy heights of Steamboat Rocks, a train of many splendors not the least of which were the wild and lonely countryside through which much of its run was made. *(Wyoming State Historical Department.)*

By 1918 when the westbound *Overland* paused at Rawlins, the necessities of wartime had increased its head-end revenue cars and apparently eliminated the traditional baggage-buffet, but it still was a train of Pullman consequence as it stopped at Granger, Wyoming, *(right)* where the rails to Oregon, shown at the extreme right of the photograph, diverged from the Overland Route past a double spouted water tank. Hostilities, too, for a time eliminated the train's observation car shown as it neared Ogden in Weber Canyon, scene of "The 1,000 Mile Tree" in construction days of the distant sixties. *(Above and Left: Fred Jukes; Opposite: Wyoming State Historical Department.)*

Switchers and road engines waited assignment in a wide variety of types and classes in Cheyenne yards in 1908, while Cheyenne depot *(below)* with its characteristic campanile was a landmark easily identified by railroaders and travelers everywhere west of Chicago. *(Two photos: Wyoming State Historical Department.)*

Eastbound out of Cheyenne yards in the year 1910 at 8:30 a.m. with the sun directly on its smokebox, the august *Overland*, candy train of the run, waits while Train No. 18, *The Oregon-Washington Limited*, running off schedule, runs around it in the hope of making up time before reaching Omaha. At the left the insigne of *The Overland*, electrically illuminated, first rode the roof of the observation car before the drumhead train herald was invented. *(Two Photos; Wyoming State Historical Department.)*

Overstuffed easy chairs, high button shoes, black silk or bombazine traveling skirts and outsize antimacassars characterized the good life aboard *The Overland's* observation cars in the era of 1905, with Fred the porter at hand when highballs were in request or the bound copies of *Munsey's Magazine* and *The Outlook*, a high toned periodical for which The President of the United States *(opposite)* often wrote book reviews. Double heading *The Overland* westbound out of Cheyenne was from earliest times taken for granted and in 1940 first No. 27 rolled splendidly toward Sherman Summit in the grand manner behind two 800 class engines. When President Roosevelt in 1902 toured the West, his private car *Rocket* was, in the natural order of things, attached to *The Overland.* *(Above: Southern Pacific; Opposite, Top: Richard Kindig; Below: Brown Bros.)*

At Lodge Pole, Nebraska, *The Overland Limited* with Union Pacific Atlantic No. 11 on the headend, has a meet in 1907 with an eastbound freight and picks up speed for the run to Sunol, next station down the line. The Harriman program of rehabilitation is still in progress and new iron is being laid on the passing track. On the opposite page are three club car interiors of equipment specially outshopped by Pullman for the North Western for service in *The Overland* in 1911 at a time when taste in railroad decor was less ornate than it had been a decade previous and when the word "Palace" was in decline. Chaste but substantial upholstery had replaced the ball fringes and potted plants of yesterday, but the bronze cuspidor was the hallmark still of cars reserved for masculine occupancy. (*Above: Wyoming State Historical Department; Opposite, Three Photos: North Western Railway.*)

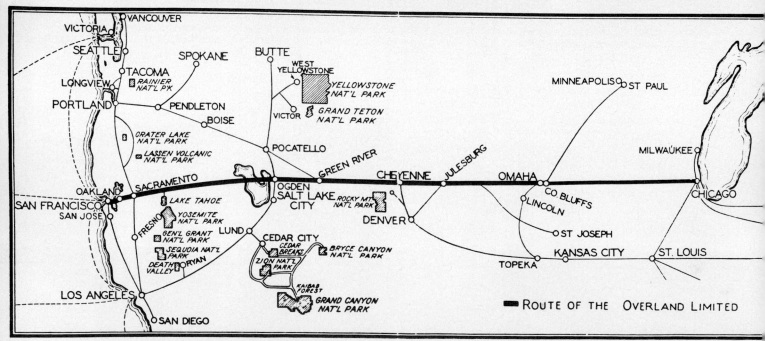

ROUTE OF THE OVERLAND LIMITED

In the early thirties *The Overland*, shown above eastbound with the identifying campanile of Cheyenne depot in the background, acknowledged hard times by including a coach in its otherwise impeccably all-Pullman consist. Public cars, buffet diner and observation, were air conditioned. So was a single through sleeper for San Francisco. Open platform observation cars lasted, of course, until the 1941 war. No self-respecting train was without one. *(Opposite: South Pacific; Above: Richard H. Kindig.)*

No. 27—San Francisco Overland Limited. Daily.
Tables A and C.

Club Car...................Chicago to San Francisco (Barber, valet and bath).
(Air-cooled.)

Observation Sleeping Car..Chicago to San Francisco—3-Compartments, 2-Drawing-rooms (S. P. 27 beyond Ogden); (Maid service and hair-dresser).
(Air-cooled.)

Standard Sleeping Cars.....Chicago to San Francisco—6-Compartments, 3-Drawing-rooms. (Air-cooled.) (S. P. 27 beyond Ogden.)

Chicago to San Francisco — 12 - Sections, Drawing-room, Compartments (S. P. 27 beyond Ogden).

Chicago to San Francisco—14-Sections (S. P. 27 beyond Ogden).

St. Louis to San Francisco—12-Sections, Drawing-room (Wabash 9 to Kansas City, U. P. 101-127 to Ogden; S. P. 27 beyond).

Salt Lake City to San Francisco—12-Sections, Drawing-room (No. 131 to Ogden, S. P. No. 27 beyond).

Tourist Sleeping Car.......Kansas City to San Francisco—16-Sections (No. 101-127 to Ogden; S. P. No. 27 beyond).

Coach.....................Chicago to San Francisco (S. P. 27).

Dining Car................Serving all meals between Chicago and San Francisco
(Air-cooled.)
A la carte service; also club breakfasts, 50c. to $1.00; table d'hote luncheons, 75c. and $1.00; table d'hote dinners, $1.00 and $1.25.

So great was the magic in the name "Overland" that the competing Atchison, Topeka & Santa Fe Railroad for several years scheduled a rival *Overland Limited* between Chicago and Los Angeles, creating some confusion and placing two trains of identical designation in service on parallel routes. Here the Santa Fe's *Overland Limited* is shown paused at the depot at Pasadena, California, handily adjacent to the Green Hotel, one of the massive resort hostels for which Pasadena was becoming noted toward the end of the nineteenth century. The photograph was taken by the celebrated William Henry Jackson of Denver and is from the archives of the State Historical Society of Colorado. At the left is the trademark of The Overland Cigar sold by the patriarchal firm of S.S. Pierce in far-off Boston, one more testimonial to the radiant celebrity of *The Overland Limited.* (S.S. Pierce.)

In the mid-twenties which were the golden noontide of *The Overland Limited*, the Burlington Railroad had the effrontery to schedule an almost identically named train, *The Overland Express* on the daily run between Chicago and Denver via Omaha. Here it is depicted in a wash drawing by Howard Fogg paused in the Iowa night on the classic run between Lake Michigan and the Queen City of the Plains.

When *The San Francisco Overland*, shown here running double headed with seventeen cars near Sherman Summit, was predominantly a military train during the years of the 1941 war, it often ran in two sections with the maximum tonnage capacity of two of the Union Pacific's powerful 800 class engines. There were sometimes more than forty train movements a day across Sherman and train crews didn't bother to change the smokebox numbers on helper engines as is evident on No. 802 in this picture. During the war years some of the luxury trimmings depicted in the promotion montage opposite, notably the barber shop, shower bath and open platform observation car lounge, were temporarily abated. *(Below: Richard H. Kindig; Opposite: Grahame Hardy Collection.)*

ALL THE COMFORTS OF A FINE HOTEL ON SOUTHERN PACIFIC

At the top of the page opposite, No. 27 passes the gravel pits on Sherman Hill near Buford with No. 7039 and No. 800 on the smoky end at fifty miles an hour in 1951. Below, with Diesel a reality for road service on the U.P., steam was still needed for the grade on Sherman for many years. *(Two Photos: Richard Kindig.)*

Here *The Overland* eastbound, No. 28, drops down the long grade from Sherman Hill into the yards at Cheyenne in September 1937 behind a giant 4-6-6-4 Challenger type engine just as a yard switcher backs out into the main line in preparation for the day's work in what was once one of the busiest railroad yards in the West. *(Richard Kindig.)*

On the opposite page are two interior views of the gentlemen's smoking and washroom of the Pullman-built Palace Sleeping Car *Topeka*, assigned to *The Overland* in the early nineties with the Union Pacific as the leasing carrier. In an age when Palace cars ranged in variety of interior decor from Egyptian to Balkan Gothic and from Renaissance baroque to French Empire, a Moorish interior suggestive of Mecca in the days of the caravan trade with Byzantine arches and ball fringed portieres raised no eyebrows. One of the interiors depicted opposite was shown in color in a company pamphlet for 1896 indicating that the seat cushions were lavender, the wall panels and carved work a subdued pink and the ceiling motif was in robin's egg blue and gold leaf. *(Two Photos: Pullman Standard.)*

When the below photograph of *The Overland Limited* as a property of the Chicago & North Western Railway was taken in 1897 en route to its Union Pacific connection at Omaha, the North Western was a Vanderbilt railroad and, like all Vanderbilt carriers since the days of the Commodore himself, it had purchased all its luxury equipment, sleeping cars, diners and buffets from the Wagner Palace Carbuilding Company. Shown above is the North Western's handsome Wagner Buffet Car No. 186 in a builder's photograph indicating that it was built from Plan A-323 in August 1897 as time was running out for the Wagner name. It appears again below directly behind the North Western's engine No. 91. *(Above: Arthur D. Dubin Collection; Below: Everett De Golyer Collection.)*

Imperial :: Palace :: Dining :: Cars

BRUNSWICK   DELMONICO
LELAND   ILLINOIS

WINE LIST.

CHAMPAGNE.

	Pts.	Qts.
Chapin & Gore's Best, half pints, $1.00.		$3.50
Piper Heidsieck,	$2.00	3.50
G. H. Munn's Extra Dry,	2.00	3.50
Pommery Sec,	2.00	3.50
Louis Roederer,	2.00	3.50
Dry Monopole,	2.00	3.50
Cook's Imperial,	1.50	2.50

SAUTERNE.

Bommes,	.75	1.25
Latour Blanche, bottled at the Chateau, 1870,	1.50	2.50

CLARET.

St. Julien, Imperial,	.50	1.50
Pontet Canet,	1.00	2.00
Medoc,	1.00	2.00

BROCTON (Chautauqua Co., N. Y.) WINES.

Sparkling, Diamond Wedding,	1.00	2.00
Sparkling, Imperial,	1.00	2.00
Still, Catawba,	.50	1.00
Still, Claret,	.50	.75
Still, Iona,	.50	1.00
Still, Regina,	.50	1.00
Still-sweet, Sunny Side,	.50	.75
Still-sweet, Isabella,	.50	.75
Still-sweet, Catawba,	.50	1.00
Still-sweet, Port,	.75	1.50
Still-sweet, Regina,	.75	1.50
Still-sweet, Sherry,	.75	1.25

WINES, LIQUORS, ETC.

Vin Ordinaire, (very good)		half pint, .15
Sour Mash Whisky, 1867,		2.50
Amontillado Sherry, Superior,		2.00
Bass' Pale Ale,	1.00	
Guinness' Dublin Porter,		.40
Ginger Ale,		.35
Congress Water,		.25
Apollinaris Water,		.25
Milwaukee Lager Beer,		.15
Budweiser Lager Beer, (very fine)		.30
Old Holland Gin,	half pint flask,	.50
Old Sour Mash Bourbon,		.50
Old Sour Mash Bourbon,		1.00
Old Coleq. Pere & Fils Brandy, 1802,	half	1.00
Old Coleq. Pere & Fils Brandy, 1802,		2.00
Old Martel Brandy,	half	.75
Old Martel Brandy,		1.50

Imported Cigars, very fine, 15c, 20c, 25c.   Cigarettes, bunch, 15c.

Imperial :: Palace :: Dining :: Cars

BRUNSWICK   DELMONICO
LELAND   ILLINOIS

DINNER.

Oysters on Half Shell.

POTAGES.

Green Sea Turtle.   Clam Chowder.

HOT ENTREES.

Sweet Breads, Braized with Mushrooms.
Lamb Cutlets, a la Soubise.   Charlotte of Apples, a la Parisienne.
Young Chickens, Sautes a l'Augerienne.   Frogs' Legs, Fried in Butter.
Soft Shell Crabs, Fried with Parsley.   Calf's Brains, Scrambled with Drawn Butter.

COLD ENTREES.

Boned Turkey.   Breast of Chicken.   Lambs' Tongues.
Lobster Salad.   Bread of Fowls' Liver, a la American.   Potato Salad.

ROASTS.

English Rib Ends of Beef.   Beef.   Young Turkey, Cranberry Sauce.
Stuffed Young Chicken.   Loin of Veal, Macedonian Style.
Saddle of Southdown Mutton, with Red Currant Jelly.
Louisville Ham, with Champagne Sauce.
Spring Lamb, Mint Sauce.   Domestic Duck.

GAME.

Saddle of Venison, with Currant Jelly.   Red Head and Canvas Back Duck with Jelly.
Illinois-Grouse, with Jelly.   Broiled Quail on Toast.
Roast Young Prairie Chicken, with Grape Jelly.
Broiled Young Pigeon.

VEGETABLES.

Baked Sweet Potatoes.   French Asparagus.   Fried Parsnips.
Boiled New Irish Potatoes.   Mashed Irish Potatoes.   Green Peas.
Stewed Tomatoes.   Lima Beans.   Green Corn.
Spring Beets.   Sliced Tomatoes,   Sliced Cucumbers.

PASTRY.

Peach Pie.   Apple Pie.   Cocoanut Pie.

PUDDINGS.

English Plum Pudding, Rum Sauce.   Golden Custard Pudding, with Preserves.

SMALL PASTRY.

Marble Cake.   Chocolate Cake.   Lady Fingers.   Egg Kisses.
Lady Cake.   Catiline Cake.   Black Cake.

DESSERT.

Vanilla Ice Cream.   Frozen Roman Punch.   Pine Apple Sherbet.
Almonds.   Pecans.   Layer Raisins.   Figs.
Brazil Nuts.   English Walnuts.   Filberts.
Bananas.   Oranges.   Apples.

English Breakfast Tea.   MEALS, 75c.   French Coffee.

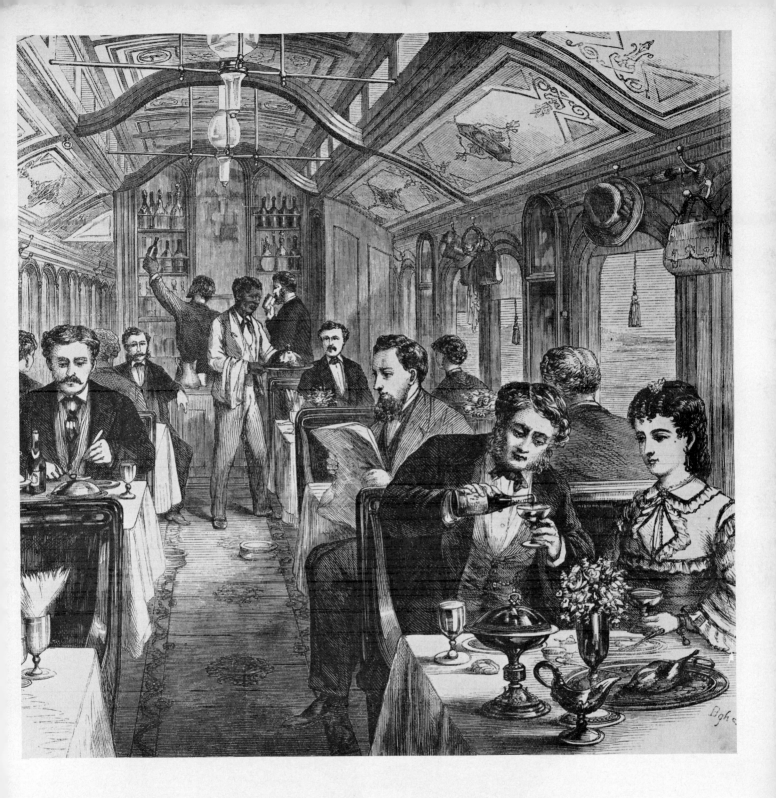

The truly remarkable menu and wine card reproduced on the page opposite from the collection of Alfred W. Johnson were not evoked by any special occasion or holiday, but were the regularly available food and drink supplied by the Chicago & North Western Railway diners on the Chicago-Omaha run in 1887, the year *The Overland Flyer* came into existence. Seasons of special rejoicing such as Christmas called for a vastly enlarged bill of fare almost invariably including roast suckling pig, which was listed on *The Overland Limited* Christmas dinner for 1913 at sixty-five cents, English plum pudding, two bits and Special Overland Punch "With Our Compliments." Until the first World War game was still plentiful and in the same year *The Overland* afforded broiled teal duck, sixty-five cents and, the most costly item on the menu, roast mallard duck at $1.25. In 1913 seven brands of champagne were available, the same number as in 1887, but the price of a half bottle in most cases had advanced from $2 to $2.50. The dining car scene on the Overland Route depicted above antedated *The Overland Flyer* by approximately a decade, but suggests the emphasis which from the beginning was laid on ample table fare for passengers bound for California.

In the first decade of its existence *The Overland Limited* made a magnificent picture of railroading in its golden age as one of the Chicago & North Western's sightly, high wheeled Atlantics rolled it through a pastoral setting of Iowa countryside. Between Chicago and Omaha, the North Western's left hand operations and celebrated dining car service were part of a rich dairyland operation in the American heartland that has been caught atmospherically in a watercolor by Howard Fogg, dean of contemporary railroad artists. Here is depicted a handsome baggage-buffet combine built to the order of the North Western in 1911 for special assignment to *The Overland Limited*. One of its features was a decor which included a Pintsch gas reading lamp between each two armchairs as well as the conventional clerestory illumination. *The Overland* was a train in which were gathered and multiplied all the amenities of luxury travel. (Two Photos: Pullman Standard.)

The great style that characterized *The Overland* in its glory years is suggested by the Pullman buffet and observation cars shown here built to the specifications of the North Western and carrying the railroad's insigne as well as the legend of *The Overland Limited* to whose service they were exclusively assigned. *(Right: Union Pacific; Below, Two Photos: Pullman Standard.)*

Until the construction of the present North Western depot in Chicago, *The Overland* sailed from the older station shown above with the train shed and converging tracks that had been landmarks since the eighties. Below, in 1928, Train No. 28 passes through Geneva, Illinois, running, in the North Western's characteristic style, on the left hand track. *(Above: Chicago & North Western; Below: A. W. Johnson.)*

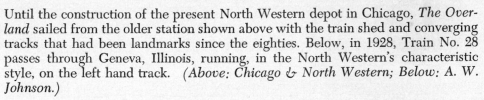

The Overland scenes and atmosphere illustrating these two pages cover a range in time of approximately a decade and a half, the oldest of them being the ornate menu cover reproduced on the opposite page which dates from the eighties when the train was new and the North Western's Chicago depot exterior in 1890 when it was well established and rapidly becoming institutional. The other three, including the dollar dinner menu at the immediate right and the touching scene depicted above of the system's only lady station-master in purposeful pose at Clinton, Iowa, date from approximately 1906 when *The Overland Limited* was a household name everywhere in the United States. The composite photo-lithograph of the train itself in a representative and pastoral North Western setting was the official company picture of the train at this time. It embraces an actual photograph superimposed on a granger setting of dairyland activities with a stand of greenery drawn in at the lower left for esthetic reasons of composition. *(Above and Right: Chicago & North Western; Three Other Pictures: A. W. Johnson Collection.)*

page 150

THE OVERLAND LIMITED

FINEST & FASTEST

Celery, en Branche	Salted Pecans

Essence of Beef, en Tasse

Chicken Okra, Southern Style

Pompano, Orleanaise
Waffle Potatoes

Patties of Lake Shrimp, Newburg

Larded Sirloin of Beef, Jardinière

Steamed Potatoes	Fried Egg Plant

Roast Teal, Fried Hominy, Currant Jelly

Hearts of Lettuce, French Dressing

Tapioca Pudding, Vanilla Sauce

Ice Cream	Assorted Cakes

Fresh Fruits

Cheese	Toasted Crackers

Demi-Tasse

DINNER $1.00

Overland Limited

is making history. It gives a maximum of extra comforts for a minimum extra fare, $10. Business men en route can keep in close touch with important happenings of the world as well as their individual business. This train

Saves a Business Day

between Chicago and San Francisco. It is a business man's train, with all the comforts and conveniences of one's own club. The new time schedule is 64 hours and 30 minutes. Leaves Chicago daily at 7 p. m., from the new Passenger Terminal, Madison and Canal Streets, arrives San Francisco 9:30 a. m. third day.

It is the only exclusively first-class train, Chicago to San Francisco. The only daily extra-fare train, Chicago to California. It is a new train of new all-steel cars, with roomy berths, spacious drawing-rooms and compartments, barber shop, baths, stenographer, valet, ladies' maid, and excellent dining-car service.

Over a magnificent double-track system of 100-lb. steel rails, ballasted with Dustless Sherman Gravel, guarded every inch of the way by Automatic Electric Block Safety Signals.

Chicago and North Western—
Union Pacific—Southern Pacific
STANDARD ROUTE OF THE WEST
Direct Route to the Panama-Pacific Exposition, 1915
For Tickets, Reservations and Full Particulars, Apply to
Chicago and North Western Ry.
A. C. JOHNSON, *Passenger Traffic Manager*   C. A. CAIRNS, *Gen'l Passenger and Ticket Agent*
Chicago, Ill.

OL2735

When the Panama-Pacific Exposition opened in San Francisco in 1915, the carriers handling *The Overland* made a special bid for the de luxe trade across the continent and took many thousands of visitors to the Golden Gate with pleasure and profit for all concerned. The $10 surcharge, a not inconsiderable sum in those halcyon days, restricted patronage to the socially and economically acceptable well-to-do and *The Overland* provided as well the fastest passage for those whose time was valuable. It was a last brief interlude of splendor before the 1914 war, already under way in Europe, was to engulf the United States and so downgrade railroad travel in America that it was to be half a decade before it recovered its former style. Opposite, *The Overland's* stately observation car *Forrest Lane*, when it paused at Council Bluffs in 1921 for a handsome portrait by Homer O. Frohart, stopped traffic at an adjacent grade crossing. Below, No. 2 rolls smokily through Winfield, Illinois, in 1929 on the North Western in a typical left hand operation. *(Above: A. W. Johnson Collection; Opposite: William Kratville Collection, A. W. Johnson.)*

The upper picture on this page shows *The Overland* early in its career in 1902 on the Chicago & North Western passing under the single track bridge of the Wisconsin Central in River Forest, Illinois. Below No. 2 rolls into Chicago yards in 1916 with the Pullman sleepers *Portslade* and *Elkington* and the observation car *Cedar Point*. Opposite *The Overland*, in May 1938, rides out of Omaha behind green and gold Hudson No. 4005, while below, in Standard steel days, it heads west out of Chicago in a typical North Western left hand operation. *(Above, Opposite: Richard H. Kindig; Three Other Photos: Alfred W. Johnson.)*

INDEX